BORN Y

COMEDY IN THREE ACTS

BY **GARSON KANIN**

★

★

DRAMATISTS
PLAY SERVICE
INC.

TO RUTH

BORN YESTERDAY

was presented by Max Gordon at the Lyceum Theatre, New York City, on February 4, 1946. It was staged by the author. Donald Oenslager designed the setting, and Miss Holliday was dressed by Mainbocher.

The cast was as follows:

BILLIE DAWN .... Judy Holliday
HARRY BROCK .... Paul Douglas
PAUL VERRALL .... Gary Merrill
ED DEVERY .... Otto Hulett
SENATOR NORVAL HEDGES .... Larry Oliver
MRS. HEDGES .... Mona Bruns
EDDIE BROCK .... Frank Otto
THE ASSISTANT MANAGER .... Carroll Ashburn
HELEN .... Ellen Hall
A BELLHOP .... William Harmon
ANOTHER BELLHOP .... Rex King
A BARBER .... Ted Mayer
A MANICURIST .... Mary Laslo
A BOOTBLACK .... Parris Morgan
A WAITER .... C. L. Burke

———————

ASSISTANT TO MR. KANIN .... Hal Gerson
COSTUMES (OTHER THAN MISS HOLLIDAY'S) .... Ruth Kanin
PRODUCTION STAGE MANAGER .... David M. Pardoll
STAGE MANAGER .... William Harmon
UNDERSTUDIES .... { Adele Robertson
                                                 James Daly

The scene is Washington, D.C.
Time : 1946
ACT ONE: September
ACT TWO: About two months later
ACT THREE: Late that night

BORN YESTERDAY

ACT ONE

SCENE: *This happens in the sitting room of Suite 67D, a large part of the best hotel in Washington, D.C. 67D is so called because it is a duplex apartment occupying the sixth and seventh floor of Wing D. It is a masterpiece of offensive good taste, colorful and lush and rich. C. a circular staircase and balcony. On balcony a huge ottoman and two doors which lead to bedroom suites. In C. of R. wall is an ornate fireplace, complete with andirons, logs, etc., and flanked on either side by a small, decorative chair. On mantel of fireplace is an antique vase, empty. Directly over fireplace unit is a large mirror in an elaborate gilt frame. There are glass light-brackets above and on either side of fireplace. Upstage of fireplace is a swinging door which leads to service wing. This door has a stop on its lower downstage corner so that it can be left open when necessary. In up R. corner a Swedish modern sideboard. The two main doors are in U.L.C. wall, opening on stage. On either side of doors is a high-backed chair. The area from balcony to L. wall is a platform 14 inches high and 5 feet deep with two steps on the D.S. edge, leading into room.*

Directly below L. side of platform is a bookcase unit, empty. Back of bookcase and out of sight of audience is a small rack on which hats are placed. L. side of stage consists of a large circular window with drapes and curtains, and two French doors leading to terrace. In the distance the Capitol dome can be seen. D.L.C. are a Lawson-type sofa and coffee table. L. of sofa is an end table, with drawer. D.R.C. is a single pedestal, ornate round table. L. of table, an arm-chair. R. of table, a straight-back chair and up-stage of table a small satin chair. On table there is a gilded telephone.

AT RISE: *It is nine P.M. The main doors are open, as are doors on balcony, U.R.C. Up R.C., in front of balcony steps is a chambermaid's cleaning unit, which consists of a rolling platform with a cabinet for clean linens in C. of it, and a large cloth bag on each end for dirty linen. It also contains a broom, dust-pan, whisk-broom and feather duster.*

Telephone on table is ringing as curtain rises. On second ring, a maid (HELEN) comes in from service wing, carrying a vase of lilies of the valley. She crosses L. and sets vase on end-table L. of sofa, then goes off to service wing. She passes the ringing phone, looks at it, but does not condescend to answer it. On fourth ring a MAN in hall walks by open door. HE looks in, but passes. Phone rings once more, then stops. A moment later, MAN returns and stands in doorway, then comes into room, looks around, picks up matches from top of bookcase U.L.C., and lights cigarette with them. This is PAUL VERRALL, of the New Republic's Washington staff. VERRALL is in his middle thirties, personable, alert, energetic. HE has a tendency to take things, and himself, too seriously. HE knows this. HE carries two books, a copy of The New Republic and some newspapers. HE wears eyeglasses. HELEN comes in from service wing, carrying five ashtrays, as HE lights his cigarette.

PAUL. Who's coming in here, Helen, do you know?

HELEN. (*Crossing to end-table L.*) Hello, Mr. Verrall. No, I don't.

PAUL. A Harry Brock, by any chance?

HELEN. I'm not the room clerk, please.

PAUL. . . . supposed to meet this guy, that's all. I wondered if maybe he was coming in here. (HELEN *looks at card stuck in among flowers.*)

HELEN. Brock.

PAUL. (*Looking around.*) I figured.

HELEN. Who's Brock?

PAUL. *Harry* Brock.

HELEN. (*Putting card back into flowers.*) Never heard of him.

PAUL. You will, Helen. Big man. Ran a little junk yard into fifty million bucks, with no help from anyone or anything—except World War II.

HELEN. Anybody checks into 67D I got no desire to meet. Believe me.

PAUL. Why not?

HELEN. Listen, you know what they charge for this layout? (*About to continue, impressively, when* PAUL *interrupts.*)
PAUL. Two hundred and thirty-five a day.
HELEN. Who told you?
PAUL. Frank.
HELEN. Oh.
PAUL. What about it?
HELEN. (*Placing ashtray on coffee table.*) Listen, anybody's got two hundred and thirty-five a day to spend on a hotel room there oughta be a law.
PAUL. . . . too many laws already.
HELEN. (*Crossing to table* D.R.C.) While I'm getting eighteen a week I don't see why anybody should spend two hundred and thirty-five a day.
PAUL. . . . for a hotel room.
HELEN. (*Placing ashtray on table.*) That's what I say.
PAUL. (*Smiling.*) I know some people who'd call you a Communist.
HELEN. (*Crossing to fireplace, placing ashtray. Darkly.*) Tell 'em I'm thinkin' about it. Seriously. (PAUL *is at window, looking out over the city.* HELEN *crosses* U.L.) Changed much, you think?
PAUL. What?
HELEN. (*Placing ashtray on bookcase.*) Washington?
PAUL. Not enough. I could stand a little more change. The idea of the war wasn't to leave everything the same, you know.
HELEN. . . . trouble with you, Mr. Verrall, you think too much. Most fellas your age get more—(SHE *breaks off abruptly as* BELL- HOP *enters, carrying two large suitcases, overnight bag and a jewel box.* HE *has a large ring with a hotel pass key around his neck.* HE *is followed by* EDDIE BROCK, *who is* HARRY BROCK'S *cousin—and servant—carrying a large leather liquor case and an old Gladstone suitcase.* SECOND BELLHOP *follows* EDDIE, *carrying* BROCK'S *luggage—two large suitcases and a two-suiter.*)
EDDIE. This stays down. The rest goes up. (EDDIE *crosses* R., *sets bag near fireplace, liquor box on floor below sideboard* U.R.)
BELLHOP. Yes, sir. (*Goes upstairs and into upstage room.* SECOND BELLHOP *follows, goes into other room.* HELEN *pulls her cleaning unit out service door and goes.* PAUL *is on his way out. As* HE *reaches door, however, he steps aside.* HARRY BROCK *stamps in, followed by* ASSISTANT MANAGER. *He wears his hat, carries a camelhair coat. Then* BILLIE DAWN *appears.* BROCK *is a huge man*

9

in his early forties. Gross is the word for him. BILLIE *is breath-takingly beautiful and breathtakingly simple.*)

ASSISTANT MANAGER. (*Proudly.*) Here we are! (BROCK *and* BILLIE *are looking around.* BILLIE *wears a mink coat and carries another. Also a large box of candy and an armful of movie magazines.* BROCK *is impressed by the room, but tries to conceal it.* HE *sees* PAUL, *but does not particularly notice him.*)

BROCK. (*Without enthusiasm. Crossing* R. *to fireplace.*) It's all right. (BILLIE *stands in front of chair* R. *of main door.* EDDIE *takes* BROCK'S *coat and hat and puts them on chair at fireplace.*)

ASSISTANT MANAGER. (*Pointing off* R.) Service wing. (*Pointing off* L.) Terrace. (*Going toward staircase.*) And the bedchambers are right this way. (HE *goes up.* BILLIE *follows.* EDDIE *is unpacking bottles of liquor from leather box and putting them on sideboard* U.R. PAUL *is still present.* BROCK *crosses to sofa, sits and takes off one shoe.*)

PAUL. (*A step forward to* R. *of sofa, extending his hand.*) Hello, Mr. Brock.

BROCK. (*Brusquely, ignoring* PAUL'S *hand.*) How are ya? (HE *turns away.* PAUL *shrugs and leaves.* BROCK *removes his other shoe. A sudden glance at door.*) Who the hell was that?

EDDIE. Search me.

BROCK. What kinda a joint is this, people in and outa your place all the time? (ASSISTANT MANAGER *returns.*)

ASSISTANT MANAGER. Mrs. Brock seems delighted with the bedchambers.

BROCK. It's not Mrs. Brock! (FIRST BELLHOP *comes down and* EDDIE *tips him as he reaches first step.*)

ASSISTANT MANAGER. (*A gulp.*) I see.

BROCK. All right Just don't get nosey. (FIRST BELLHOP *closes main doors and goes.*)

ASSISTANT MANAGER. Not at all.

BROCK. There ain't no Mrs. Brock except my mother and she's dead.

ASSISTANT MANAGER. I see.

BROCK. (*Snapping fingers. To* EDDIE.) Eddie! . . . Take care of 'im. (ASSISTANT MANAGER *turns to* EDDIE. EDDIE *comes over, reaches into pocket, takes out roll of bills. Looks at* BROCK. THEY *reach a swift, silent, understanding as to how much.* EDDIE *hands* ASSISTANT MANAGER *two ten dollar bills.*)

ASSISTANT MANAGER. (*To* EDDIE.) Thank you. (*Then, to* BROCK.)

That is, thank *you*. So much. (SECOND BELLHOP *comes down*, EDDIE *tips him as he goes.*)

BROCK. (*Loud and fast.*) All right, all right. Just listen. Anybody works in this room just tell 'im to do it good and do it quick and nobody'll get hurt. I'm a big tipper, tell 'em, and I don't like a lotta people around all the time and I don't like to wait for nothin'. I ain't used to it.

ASSISTANT MANAGER. I'm sure everything will be just that, Mr. Brock. (HE *bows, low.*)

BROCK. (*With a backhand wave.*) Okay! Knock off! (ASSISTANT MANAGER *is caught at the bottom of his bow. Straightens up, awkwardly.*)

ASSISTANT MANAGER. Thank you *very* much, Mr. Brock. (HE *leaves.*)

BROCK. (*Rising and shouting.*) Billie! (*Buzzer sounds.*)

BILLIE. (*Appearing on balcony, echoing his tone.*) What?

BROCK. (*Indicating room.*) Not bad, huh?

BILLIE. (*Without enthusiasm, circling ottoman.*) It's all right. (EDDIE *crosses* L. *to door.*)

BROCK. (*Sore.*) All right, she says! You know what this place costs a day?

BILLIE. (*Still moving.*) Two thirty-five. You told me. (SHE *leaves, with a bored wave of her hips.* BROCK *walks back to sofa and sits. Takes off tie.* EDDIE *opens door.* ED DEVERY *comes in, slightly drunk.*)

DEVERY. Hello, Eddie.

EDDIE. Hello. (*About* ED DEVERY. *Thirty years ago, when he was secretary to a great Supreme Court Justice, he was known as a young man destined for greatness. The white star shone clearly on his forehead. Fifteen years later, he was still so known except to himself.* HE *knew then that he had lost his way. Now everyone knows. They speak of his past brilliance in law and charitably forget that he now has but one client,* HARRY BROCK, *who might have difficulty in finding a reputable lawyer to serve him. But* ED DEVERY *is past caring. Brock represents over $100,000 a year, which buys plenty of the best available Scotch.* HE *puts his hat and briefcase on chair* R. *of door.*)

DEVERY. (*To* BROCK, *as he comes down into room.*) Welcome to our city.

BROCK. Yeah.

EDDIE. (*Following* DEVERY.) Say, I got this ticket to be fixed.

11

(Reaches into his pocket, searching for it.)
DEVERY. *(Annoyed.)* What's it about?
EDDIE. Ah, some louse just as we blew into town. Here. *(Hands over pink traffic summons.)*
DEVERY. *(Loud because irritated)* I should like to impress one thing on your non-existent intellect—the fact that I am a lawyer does not mean that I own the law.
EDDIE. *(Outraged innocence.)* What'd *I* do? What'd I *do?*
DEVERY. *(Resigned.)* All right. I'll see what I can manage. *(Takes deep, weary breath, puts traffic ticket in pocket. EDDIE goes to sideboard.)*
BROCK. *(To DEVERY.)* You plastered again?
DEVERY. *(With a smiling little shake of his head.)* Still.
BROCK. I told you I got a couple things can't wait.
DEVERY. Don't worry about me, massa, I can see a loophole at twenty paces.
BROCK. What'd we make out?
DEVERY. *(Crossing L. to BROCK.)* . . . going to be all right. May cost slightly more than we estimated, but no cause for alarm.
BROCK. *(Suspicious.)* How much more?
DEVERY. It's negligible.
BROCK. Why more?
DEVERY. Supply and demand, Harry. Crooks are becoming rare in these parts. Therefore they come high. Don't worry.
BROCK. What do you mean, don't worry? This kinda stuff ain't deductible, y'know.
DEVERY. *(Thinks a moment, smiling, then crossing c.s.)* I'm not so sure. Perhaps we should make a trial issue of it. *(As though dictating.)* "Item: one bribe, $80,000."
BROCK. *(Outraged.)* Eighty? *(Phone rings.)*
DEVERY. *(Turning to BROCK.)* What's the matter? *(EDDIE crosses to phone.)*
BROCK. You said—uh—negligible.
DEVERY. . . . figured fifty, didn't we?
EDDIE. *(Answering phone.)* Yeah?
BROCK. *(To DEVERY.)* You're very handy with *my* dough, you know it?
EDDIE. *(On phone.)* . . . Yeah, he is. Who wants 'im? . . . Wait a second. *(To DEVERY.)* Some guy for *you.* Verrall. *(BROCK chews on match-stick petulantly.)*
DEVERY. *(Going to phone.)* Thanks. *(Takes phone from EDDIE.*

12

EDDIE *takes* BROCK'S *coat and hat, and his own suitcase into service wing.* DEVERY, *into phone.*) How are you, Paul? . . . Good . . . . How's the crusade business? (*He laughs at* PAUL'S *reply.*) . . . Sure, any time now. Sooner the better. Fine. . . . See you. . . . (*Hangs up.*)

BROCK. What's all that?

DEVERY. Paul Verrall. I told you about him.

BROCK. I don' remember no Verrall.

DEVERY. (*Crossing to* BROCK.) He's a writer. New Republic. Wants an interview. Smart boy. He's just back from a long time in Europe with lots of ideas and lots of energy.

BROCK. I don' wanna talk to no writers. I gotta get shaved.

DEVERY. I think you'd better talk to this one.

BROCK. What's so important?

DEVERY. Just do it.

BROCK. Why?

DEVERY. This is one of the few fellows in Washington to look out for. Thing to do is take him in. Then he doesn't go poking.

BROCK. (*Loud.*) Eddie!

DEVERY. How's Billie?

BROCK. She's all right. Upstairs. (EDDIE *comes in from service wing.*) Get me a shave up here.

EDDIE. (*Crossing to table* D.R.C.) Right. (*Picks up phone.*)

DEVERY. Harry——

BROCK. What?

EDDIE. (*On phone.*) Barber Shop.

DEVERY. Tell Billie to wear something nice and plain for the Senator. He may be bringing his wife.

BROCK. Tell'er yourself. You ain't pregnant.

EDDIE. (*On phone.*) This is Harry Brock's apartment. Send up a barber and a manicure. Right away. . . . Harry Brock! . . . That's right. . . . Okay, make it snappy. (*Starts to hang up.*)

BROCK. And a shine!

EDDIE. (*An overlapping echo, into phone.*) And a shine! (HB *hangs up.*) Be right up.

DEVERY. (*At* C., *lighting cigarette.*) Eddie, how would you like to save my life?

EDDIE. Soda or plain water?

DEVERY. Neat.

EDDIE. Right! (*Goes to mix drinks up* R.)

BROCK. (*Rising, removing jacket.*) Don't worry about Billie. One

13

thing, she knows how to dress. You know what it costs me for clothes for her?

DEVERY. (*Crossing down to table.*) That's not all I'm worried about, Harry.

BROCK. What? (*Tosses jacket on back of sofa.*)

DEVERY. Well, did you *have* to bring Billie?

BROCK. (*Big.*) I may be here God knows *how* long. (*Rolls up shirt sleeves.*)

DEVERY. (*Crossing to sofa.*) Trouble is, this is a city of few secrets and much chat.

BROCK. Anybody chats me I'll bust 'em in half.

DEVERY. Fine. That'll get you right where you want to go. Up with the dress-for-dinner bunch. (EDDIE *crosses* L., *bringing drink to* DEVERY, *and holding one for himself.*)

BROCK. (*Sits.*) What do I care?

DEVERY. I don't know. What *do* you care? (EDDIE *hands him drink.*) Thanks. (EDDIE *goes out to service wing, consuming his drink en route.* DEVERY *sits beside* BROCK.) Listen, Harry, you've got a chance to be one of the men who runs this country. Better than that. You can run the men who run it. It takes power. You've got some. It takes money. You've got plenty. Above all, it takes judgment and intelligence. (*A long pause.* DEVERY *calmly sips his drink.* BROCK *gets the inference with a sudden spasm.*) That's why you pay me a hundred thousand a year. (EDDIE *returns with bottle of Poland Water. He puts it on floor near sideboard.*)

BROCK. What's all the excitement?

DEVERY. Nothing. I'm just trying to make it clear where I fit in.

BROCK. You don't have to holler.

DEVERY. All right.

BROCK. (*Rising.*) Honest to God, I thought I done sump'n wrong! (HE *moves around to back of sofa, and crosses* R.)

DEVERY. (*In charge.*) When Verrall gets here, be friendly. Treat him nicely. Don't bull him. Just be yourself. Treat him like a doll you're trying to make.

BROCK. (*Whirling in his tracks, shocked.*) Wait a minute! (*Buzzer sounds,* EDDIE *starts for door.*)

DEVERY. (*Rising.*) . . . leave you alone with him. Better that way. I want to see Billie, anyway. (DEVERY *crosses to door, heading off* EDDIE *with a gesture. Admits* VERRALL. EDDIE *goes out to service wing.*) Hello, Paul.

PAUL. Ed. (THEY *shake hands.*)

14

DEVERY. (*As* PAUL *comes into room.*) Harry Brock, Paul Verrall.
PAUL. How do you do, sir? (*Bows, slightly and sharply. A habit.*
THEY *shake hands.*)
BROCK. How are ya? (*Looks at* PAUL, *quizzically.*) Ain't I see you
some place before? Lately? (PAUL *smiles.*) Excuse me for my coat
off. I have to get shaved and so forth. I hope you don't mind.
PAUL. (*To* DEVERY.) What've you been telling this guy about me?
DEVERY. If you gentlemen will excuse me——(*Goes upstairs.*)
BROCK. (*To* DEVERY.) Sure——(*To* PAUL.) siddown! What'll you
drink? (*Crosses to* R. *of table.* PAUL *sits* L. *of table.*)
PAUL. Scotch, please—if you've got it.
BROCK. (*A short laugh.*) If I got it! (*Calls out, loudly.*) Eddie!!
(*To* PAUL.) I got everything. Where you think you are? (EDDIE
comes in from service wing on the run.) Where the hell *you* been?
EDDIE. Nothing, I——
BROCK. Stick around, willya, for Christ sake an' give the man a
Scotch and—(*To* PAUL.) soda?
PAUL. Plain water.
BROCK. (*To* EDDIE.) Plain water.
EDDIE. (*To* BROCK.) Right. Rye ginger ale for you?
BROCK. Right. (EDDIE *crosses up* R. *to sideboard, mixes drinks.*
BROCK *continues to* PAUL, *happily, indicating* EDDIE *with his
thumb.*) He always knows what I feel to drink. Yeah. He's worked
for me I don't know *how* many years. Also, he's my cousin. He
knows me insides out. (*To* EDDIE.) Right?
EDDIE. (*Brightly.*) *That's* right!
PAUL. Maybe I should be interviewing Eddie. (BROCK *howls at
the idea.*)
BROCK. Hey, you maybe got sump'n there. That's pretty good.
(*Puts his foot on chair and leans toward* PAUL.) What's it gonna
be, pal? A plug or a pan?
PAUL. Why——
BROCK. I like to know these things. Then I know how to talk, if I
know your angle.
PAUL. No angle. Just, well—just the facts.
BROCK. Oh, a pan! (*Laughs, confident of his boorish charm.* EDDIE
comes down with drinks.)
PAUL. Not exactly. (*Taking drink.*) Thanks. (EDDIE *goes to liquor
case, begins unpacking cigarettes, monogrammed matchboxes and
humidor.*)
BROCK. (*To* PAUL, *picking up his drink.*) It's okay! Don' worry.

15

Write what you want. See, the way I look at it is this way. You can't hurt me, you can't help me. Nobody can. (*Raises silent toast to* PAUL. THEY *drink*.) I'm only here talkin' with you 'cause Ed Devery asked me. (EDDIE *crosses* L., *carrying humidor*.) What the hell, I pay a guy a hundred grand a year for advice so I'm a sucker if I don' take it. Right?

EDDIE. (*Automatically*.) That's right!

BROCK. (*Shouting angrily across room*.) Butt out, willya?! (EDDIE *bounces around, startled and scared, wondering what he has done to offend. He places humidor on* C. *section of bookcase, then goes back to liquor case for cigarettes.* BROCK *picks up his soft soap again and continues to* PAUL.) Devery likes it when I get wrote about. (*Goes to humidor, brings forth an individually boxed cigar*.)

PAUL. Well, of course, in Washington, Mr. Brock, there's a certain value in the right kind of——

BROCK. (*Crossing back to* PAUL *and interrupting*.) Cut it out, willya? You're breakin' my heart. Washington! I licked every town I ever decided, so what's different? (*Offering cigar to* PAUL.) Have a cigar! (EDDIE *crosses* L. *front of sofa and around back of it, putting cigarettes and matches on coffee table. Then, during following, crosses to table* R., *puts down boxes of cigarettes and matches, removes* BROCK'S *glass, and returns to sideboard*.)

PAUL. (*Taking cigar*.) Thanks. (*Looking at it carefully*.) I'll give it to a Congressman. (*Puts it in pocket*.)

BROCK. (*Crossing to* C.) Five bucks apiece they cost me. From Cuba some place.

PAUL. (*Smiling*.) Well, in that case I'll give it to a *Senator*!

BROCK. (*Thoughtfully*.) Senators're pretty big stuff around here, huh?

PAUL. Yes. (BROCK *snorts in disgust*.) Why? Shouldn't they be?

BROCK. Listen, you know what's a Senator to me? A guy who makes around two hundred bucks a week. (PAUL *smiles, takes a few sheets of folded note-paper from breast pocket, pencil from another pocket, and makes note.* BROCK *crosses* L., *sits on sofa. Lighting cigarette*.) What you puttin' in?

PAUL. (*Writing*.) Your little joke.

BROCK. (*Delighted*.) You like it, huh?

PAUL. First class.

BROCK. Maybe I oughta be on the radio!

PAUL. Maybe.

BROCK. How much you wanna bet I make more money than those Amos and Andy? (EDDIE *takes bottle of Poland Water upstairs into Brock's room*)

PAUL. No bet. (BROCK *leans back happily.* HE *feels he is doing well. He likes* PAUL. *Stretches out comfortably.*)

BROCK. (*Expansively.*) Well, fella, what d'you wanna know?

PAUL. (*Suddenly.*) How much money have you got?

BROCK. (*Startled.*) What?

PAUL. (*Rising, crossing to him.*) How much money have you got?

BROCK. (*Sitting up.*) How should I know? (*Spreading arms wide.*) What *am* I, an *accountant?*

PAUL. You don't know?

BROCK. Not exactly.

PAUL. Fifty million?

BROCK. I tell you the truth. I don' know.

PAUL. Ten million?

BROCK. Maybe.

PAUL. One million?

BROCK. More.

PAUL. (*Pressing.*) How much?

BROCK. (*With finality.*) Plenty!

PAUL. (*Giving up.*) Okay. (*Turns away, crosses back to his chair.*)

BROCK. (*Sitting up.*) And listen, I made every nickel. Nobody ever give me nothin'!

PAUL. Nice work. (*Sits.*)

BROCK. (*Rising, crossing* C.) I can tell a'ready. You're gonna give me the business.

PAUL. (*Trying to charm him.*) Wait a minute ——

BROCK. (*Overlapping.*) Go ahead. I like it.

PAUL.—You've got me wrong.

BROCK. (*Moving to* PAUL.) Go ahead! Work for me! I got more people workin' for me than knows it. (*Turns away.*)

PAUL. What's your feeling on —— ?

BROCK. (*Turning back.*) Go ahead! Pan me. Tell how I'm a mugg and a roughneck. You'll do me good.

PAUL. Listen, Mr. Brock ——

BROCK. (*Crossing* R. *to* PAUL, HE *takes off in high, gesturing graphically throughout,*) Lemme tell you about Cleveland. In 1937 there's a big dump there, see, and the city wants to get rid of it. High class scrap. So I go out there to look it over myself. There's a lots of other guys there, too. From Bethlehem even and like that.

17

I didn't have a chance and I knew it. I figure I'm outa my class and I'm all ready to pull out when all of a sudden the goddamndest thing comes out there in one of the papers. About me. A big write up. It says my name and about how come the city is gonna do business with hoodlums. Mind ya, I was outa my class. I didn't have the kinda buttons a guy needs for a deal like that. So the next day—again. This time they got a picture of me. Next thing you know, a guy calls me up. A guy from the Municipal Commission. He comes up to see me and he says they don't want no trouble. So I naturally string 'im along and I get busy on the phone and I raise some dough with a couple of boys from *De*-troit. Then comes the *big* pan. On the front page. Next day I close the deal and in a week (*Snaps his fingers.*) I'm cartin'. (EDDIE *comes down stairs, goes to sideboard.*)

PAUL. What's your point?

BROCK. (*Turning to him.*) My point is you can't do me no harm if you make me out to be a mugg. Maybe you'll help me. Everybody gets scared, and for me that's good. Everybody scares easy.

PAUL. Well, not everybody.

BROCK. Well, enough. You can't hurt me. All you can do is build me up or shut up. Have a drink. (*Snaps fingers at* EDDIE, *who comes down to table, takes* PAUL'S *glass.*)

PAUL. (*To* EDDIE.) No, thanks. Really. (EDDIE *puts glass back, starts to turn away.*)

BROCK. (*To* EDDIE, *fiercely.*) Do what I'm tellin' ya! Who the hell pays you around here? (EDDIE *bounces, takes glass, looks at* BROCK, *cowed, then goes to sideboard.* BROCK *indicates* EDDIE *and continues gently.*) When I'm home, he shaves me in the morning. I got my own barber chair. (*To* EDDIE.) Right?

EDDIE. (*As usual.*) That's right!

BROCK. (*Returning to sofa.*) Well, go ahead, pal. I thought you wanted to intraview me. (*A pause.*)

PAUL. Where were you born?

BROCK. (*Settling back.*) Jersey. Plainfield, New Jersey. I went to work when I was twelve years old and I been workin' ever since. I tell you my first job. A paper route. (*He pronounces it 'rowt.'* EDDIE *puts drink beside* PAUL.) I bought a kid out with a swift kick in the keester.

PAUL. (*Writing.*) And you've been working ever since.

BROCK. (*Missing the point.*) Right. I tell you how I'm the top man in my racket. I been in it over twenty-five years. In the same racket. (EDDIE *goes upstairs, taking liquor case into* BROCK'S *bedroom.*)

PAUL. Steel.

BROCK. Junk. Not steel. *Junk.*

PAUL. Oh.

BROCK. (*Sitting up.*) Look, don't butter me up. I'm a junk man. I ain't ashamed to say it.

PAUL. All right.

BROCK. Lemme give you some advice, sonny boy. Never crap a crapper. I can sling it with the best of 'em!

PAUL. Twenty-five years, you say?

BROCK. (*Moving to edge of sofa.*) I tell you. I'm a kid with a paper route. I got this little wagon. So on my way home nights, I come through the alleys pickin' up stuff. I'm not the only one. All the kids are doin' it. Only difference is, they keep it. Not me. I sell it. First thing you know, I'm makin' seven, eight bucks a week from that. Three bucks from papers. So I figure out right off which is the right racket. I'm just a kid, mind you, but I could see that. Pretty soon, the guy I'm sellin' to is handin' me anywheres from fifteen to twenty a week. So he offers me a job for *ten!* Dumb jerk. I'd be sellin' this guy his own stuff back half the time and he never knew.

PAUL. How do you mean?

BROCK. (*Relishing the memory.*) Well, in the night, see, I'm under the fence (*A shovel-like gesture with both hands*) and I drag it out (*He does so.*) and load up. (*Puts stuff on his back.*) In the morning (*Tracing the way with a wide arc.*) I bring it in the front way and collect! (*Pockets imaginary money, gleefully.*)

PAUL. Twelve years old, you were?

BROCK. (*Easily.*) Sump'n like that.

PAUL. So pretty soon you owned the whole yard.

BROCK. Damn right! This guy, the jerk? He works for *me* now. (*Happily.*) And you know who else works for me? That kid whose paper route I swiped. (*Magnanimously.*) I figure I owe 'im. (*Modestly.*) That's how I am.

PAUL. Pretty good years for the—junk business, these last few.

BROCK. (*With a mysterious grin.*) I ain't kickin'.

PAUL. Do you anticipate a decline now?

BROCK. (*A sudden frown.*) Talk plain, pal. (*Buzzer sounds.* EDDIE *comes downstairs to open door.*)

PAUL. (*Talking plain.*) Is it still going to be good, do you think?

19

BROCK. (*Darkly.*) We'll make it good.

PAUL. (*Quickly.*) Who's we? (BROCK *senses he is being cornered.*)

BROCK. (*Triumphantly.*) *We* is *me*, that's who!

PAUL. I see.

BROCK. Fancy talk don't go with me. (EDDIE *opens door for* BARBER, MANICURIST *and* BOOTBLACK.)

BARBER. Good evening. In here, sir?

BROCK. Yeah. (*Removes his shirt, hands it to* EDDIE. *He wears a silk undershirt. Crosses* R.)

PAUL. (*Rising and crossing* L.) Well, I'll get out of your ——

BROCK. Don't go. Siddown! Siddown! (BARBER *and* MANICURIST *go about their work.* BROCK *looks at* PAUL *and smiles.*) Siddown—I like you. You play your cards right, I'll put you on the payroll. You know what I mean? (EDDIE *takes* BROCK'S *shirt upstairs.* PAUL *sits* R. *arm of sofa.*)

PAUL. Sure.

BROCK. (*To* BARBER.) Once over easy and no talkin'. (BARBER *nods head in understanding. To* MANICURIST.) Just brush 'em up. I get a manicure every day. (*He sits.*)

MANICURIST. Yes, sir. (BOOTBLACK *gets into position with his polishing kit, then notices* BROCK'S *lack of shoes, looks up, confused.*)

BROCK. (*To* BOOTBLACK, *with an impatient motion.*) Over *there* some place! (BOOTBLACK *finds shoes on floor* R. *of sofa, picks them up, takes them, along with his equipment, upstage where he sits on second step and works.* BROCK *continues, to* PAUL.) Keep goin'. It's okay. (BARBER *puts towel around back of* BROCK'S *neck.*)

PAUL. I've been wondering what you're doing in Washington?

BROCK. (*Genially.*) None o' your goddamn business. (BARBER *starts to put hair cloth on* BROCK. EDDIE *comes downstairs and goes out to service wing.*)

PAUL. Sure it is.

BROCK. How come?

PAUL. You're a big man, Mr. Brock. (BARBER *tucks in hair cloth.*)

BROCK. (*To* BARBER, *fractiously.*) Not so tight!

BARBER. Sorry, sir.

BROCK. (*To* PAUL.) Sightseein'. That's what I'm in Washington for. Sightseein'!

PAUL. All right.

BROCK. (*Face to ceiling.*) Put that in the write-up, then nobody'll be scared. (BARBER *starts to apply brushless shaving cream to*

BROCK'S *face.*)
PAUL. How long you think you'll be around?
BROCK. (*Cute.*) Depends how many sights I got to see.
PAUL. . . . some talk you may be around for a long, long time.
BROCK. Where'd you get that?
PAUL. Around.
BROCK. Bull. What the hell do I care about politics? I got enough trouble in my own racket. I don't know nothin' about the politics racket.
PAUL. I hear you've come to find out.
BROCK. (*Still lying back, bringing a threatening hand from beneath hair cloth, pointing his finger at* PAUL *warningly.*) Listen, pal, so far I been nice to you. Don't pump me.
PAUL. My life work.
BROCK. Well, don't work on me. I like to be friends with you. (DEVERY *appears on balcony, starts down stairs.* BARBER *begins to shave* BROCK.)
DEVERY. (*To* PAUL.) How you getting on with the monarch of all he surveys?
PAUL. Great. I found out he was born in Plainfield, New Jersey. He sure is a tough man to dig. (*A grunt of disagreement from* BROCK, *as* BARBER *works on his upper lip.*)
DEVERY. I can't believe that. He loves to talk.
PAUL. Not to me.
BROCK. Why, I told you the story of my life, practically. (BILLIE *comes down stairs, crosses to sideboard.*)
PAUL. (*To* DEVERY.) He wouldn't even tell me how much money he's got.
BROCK. I don't know, I'm tellin' you.
PAUL. (*To* DEVERY.) And he wouldn't tell me what he was doing in Washington.
BROCK. Because it's none o' your business.
DEVERY. No secret. Just a little tax stuff. I told you. (BILLIE *takes bottle of liquor, starts back.*)
PAUL. I know, but I didn't believe you.
DEVERY. (*As* BILLIE *reaches stairs.*) Oh, Billie, this is my friend Paul Verrall. (*To* PAUL.) Billie Dawn.
PAUL. (*Making his habitual bow.*) How do you do? (BILLIE *acknowledges introduction with what she thinks is a curtsey. It actually is a side bump.*)
BROCK. (*Turning to look at her.*) Wait a minute! (BARBER *stops*

working and waits, razor poised.)
BILLIE. (*At foot of stairs. Slightly scared.*) What's a matter?
BROCK. Where you think you're goin' with *that*?
BILLIE. (*Casually.*) Upstairs.
BROCK. Put it back! (MANICURIST *and* BOOTBLACK *stop working as* BROCK *turns further out of position.*)
BILLIE. I just wanted ——
BROCK. (*Cutting her off sharply.*) I know what you wanted. Put it back!
BILLIE. Why can't I —— ?
BROCK. (*Mean.*) Because I say you can't, that's why. We got somebody comin'. Somebody important. I don't want you stinkin'. (*A pause.*)
BILLIE. Well, can't I just have —— ?
BROCK. No! Now put it back and go on upstairs and change your clothes and don' gimme no trouble. (BILLIE *stands motionless, humiliated.* BROCK, *in a sudden burst of impatience.*) Do what I'm tellin' ya!! (*A tense moment, then* BILLIE *obeys.* PAUL *and* DEVERY *have half turned away in embarrassment.* BROCK *settles back in his chair.* BARBER *resumes shaving.* BILLIE *has replaced bottle, then starts upstairs, her flashing eyes on* BROCK *as she ascends. Her lips form a choice collection of invective. Silence. Nobody watches her go. At top of stairs,* SHE *turns and regards* PAUL *with strange interest, but continues her move. If we were close enough we might recognize the faint beginning of a smile.* SHE *goes into her room.* EDDIE *enters from service wing, carrying pail of ice. Puts it on sideboard.*)
DEVERY. (*Crossing to* C.) Barber, what'll you take to cut his throat? (BROCK *sits up so suddenly that* BARBER *almost does so.* BROCK *rises, in a fury, whips off hair cloth, throws it on chair, crosses to* DEVERY, *towel in hand.*)
BROCK. There's some kinda jokes I don't like, Ed ——
DEVERY. Don't get excited.
BROCK. Don't tell me what to do! (*Suddenly pushes* DEVERY'S *face, hard.* DEVERY *is startled and almost falls.* PAUL *steadies him. A gasp from* MANICURIST *as the room freezes in shocked surprise.*)
DEVERY. (*Straightening up, coming back to* BROCK.) Jesus, Harry! It was just a joke.
BROCK. (*Turning to* BARBER.) That's all.
BARBER. Not quite finished, sir.

BROCK. (*Sharply.*) That's all, I told you. Beat it!

BARBER. Very good, sir.

BROCK. (*To* MANICURIST.) You, too. (*To* EDDIE, *indicating the help.*) Eddie, take care of 'em. (BARBER *and* MANICURIST *gather their equipment.* BOOTBLACK *places shoes near sideboard.* DEVERY *crosses to sideboard, pours himself a double drink.*)

PAUL. (*A step* U.C.) I guess I'd better be —— (EDDIE *tips* MANICURIST, *then* BARBER, *then* BOOTBLACK.)

BROCK. (*Crossing to* PAUL.) Don't go.

PAUL. I really should. I've got some work.

BROCK. (*Wiping his face.*) Stick around, can't you! Looks like you're about the only friend I got left around here.

PAUL. Well, I'm not far. If anyone starts beating you, just scream and I'll come running. (BROCK *laughs.* BARBER, MANICURIST *and* BOOTBLACK *leave, regarding* BROCK *expressively.* EDDIE *is clearing glasses.*)

BROCK. (*Shaking hands with* PAUL.) You live in the hotel here?

PAUL. Right down the hall.

BROCK. Fine. (EDDIE *goes out to service wing.*)

PAUL. Other side of the tracks, of course.

BROCK. Say, don't kid me. I hear you do fine.

PAUL. (*To* DEVERY.) Good night, Ed.

DEVERY. (*Quietly.*) Night. (*He drinks.*)

BROCK. (*To* PAUL.) See you soon.

PAUL. (*As* HE *leaves.*) Good night. Thanks for everything. (DEVERY *crosses up* C. *to get brief-case at door.*)

BROCK. (*Moving to back of sofa.*) Don' mention it.

DEVERY. I need Billie's signature on a few things. Eddie, too.

BROCK. (*Still wiping face.*) Sure. (*Yells.*) Billie! (DEVERY *crosses to table* R.)

BILLIE'S VOICE. What?

BROCK. Come on down here! Right away! (*To* DEVERY.) What you sore about?

DEVERY. Not sore, Harry.

BROCK. You look funny.

DEVERY. (*Opening his case.*) I know.

BROCK. Don't you feel good? You want a aspirin?

DEVERY. No, no. I'm fine. In fact, considering that I've been dead for sixteen years, I'm in remarkable health. (BILLIE *comes down, fastening cuffs of the dignified dress into which she has changed.*)

BROCK. (*To* DEVERY.) Swear to God, some time I don't understand you at all.

DEVERY. (*Smiling.*) Some time?

BILLIE. (*To* BROCK.) What do you want?

BROCK. Ed.

DEVERY. . . . few things I want you to sign, honey.

BILLIE. (*Crossing to table* R.) That's all I do around here is sign.

BROCK. Too bad about you. (*To* DEVERY.) When's he comin'? This Senator guy?

DEVERY. Any time now.

BROCK. I better get fixed up, huh? (DEVERY *nods. Still in his undershirt, and shoeless,* BROCK *picks up his jacket and tie, starts up, then stops, looks at* BILLIE. *Goes behind her, then to her* L., *examining every detail of her get-up.* SHE *follows him with her eyes.* U.L. *of table* BROCK *looks at* DEVERY, *concerned.*) She look all right to you?

BILLIE. (*Disdainfully.*) Look who's talkin'!

DEVERY. (*To* BROCK.) Perfect.

BROCK. You *sure,* now?

BILLIE. (*In a prideful whine.*) What's the matter with me? (BROCK *pays no attention to her.*)

BROCK. (*To* DEVERY, *as he goes upstairs.*) Tell me if sump'n's wrong. I don' want to start off on no left foot.

DEVERY. Don't worry. (BROCK *goes into his room.* DEVERY *brings out sheaf of legal papers, spreads them out for* BILLIE *to sign. Hands her his fountain pen.*)

BILLIE. What's got into *him?* (EDDIE *comes in from service wing, picks up* BROCK'S *shoes, goes upstairs.*)

DEVERY. Nothing. He just wants to make a good impression.

BILLIE. (*Aloof.*) So, let 'im.

DEVERY. (*Pointing out a line.*) Two places on this one, please.

BILLIE. (*Signing first document, head close to paper.*) What happened to all that stuff I signed last week?

DEVERY. (*Smiling.*) All used up.

BILLIE. I bet I signed about a million of these.

DEVERY. What you get for being a multiple corporate officer.

BILLIE. (*Signing second document.*) I *am?* (*She looks up.* DEVERY *nods.* SHE *smiles.*) What do you know!

DEVERY. . . . come a long way from the chorus, all right.

BILLIE. (*Proudly.*) I wasn't only in the chorus. In "Anything Goes" I spoke lines.

DEVERY. Really?

BILLIE. Of course. *(Signing third document.)*
DEVERY. *(As he blots second document.)* How many?
BILLIE. How many what?
DEVERY. ...lines did you speak?
BILLIE. Five. *(Thumb on pinkie.)* "Yes, I am!" *(Next finger.)* "He was here, but he's not here now!" *(Next finger, airily.)* "Oh, just a friend." *(In her most refined speech.)* "I never drink with men I don't know." *(In her normal rough voice.)* "Take off, Buster!" *(She resumes signing.)*
DEVERY. I never knew that.
BILLIE. Ask anybody.
DEVERY. I believe you.
BILLIE. *(Signing fourth document.)* I could of been a star, probably. If I'd of stuck to it.
DEVERY. Why didn't you?
BILLIE. *(Signing fifth document.)* Harry didn't want me bein' in the show. He likes to get to bed early.
DEVERY. I see.
BILLIE. *(Signing sixth document.)* He's changed, Harry. Don't you think so?
DEVERY. How?
BILLIE. I don' know. He used to be like more satisfied. Now he's always runnin' around. Like this. What'd we have to come to Washington, D.C. for?
DEVERY. *(Blotting.)* Long story.
BILLIE. Well, don't tell it to me. I don' care where he goes. I just wish he'd settle down.
DEVERY. *(Putting documents in case, bringing out more.)* Ambitious.
BILLIE. *(Signing again.)* I know. He *talks* all the time now. He never used to. Now he's got me up half the night tellin' me what a big man he is. *(Unconsciously mimicking* BROCK.*)* And how he's gonna be *bigger.* Run *everything.*
DEVERY. He may, at that.
BILLIE. *(Airily.)* Personally, I don' care one way or the other. *(She signs again.)*
DEVERY. Very few people do, that's why he may get to do it. The curse of civilization. Don't-care-ism. Satan's key to success.
BILLIE. *(Looking up at* DEVERY.*)* What kinda talk is that? You drunk or sump'n?
DEVERY. *(Blotting.)* ... drunk *and* sump'n.
BILLIE. All right. I give up. *(She puts pen down and steals look at liquor over her shoulder.* DEVERY *puts away papers.* SHE *rises, goes to sideboard, fixes drink.)*
DEVERY. *(In a warning sing-song as he crosses to chair* R *of door*

25

with brief-case.) Take it easy.

BILLIE. (*At liquor cabinet up* R.) Look now, don't *you* start.

DEVERY. Better if you drink later, Billie, after they've gone.

BILLIE. What's the deal, anyway?

DEVERY. (*Crossing back to* L. *of table.*) No deal. Just important people, that's all.

BILLIE. (U.R. *of table.*) Who? This Senator guy?

DEVERY. And *Mrs. Hedges.*

BILLIE. Harry told me this fella works for him.

DEVERY. In a way.

BILLIE. So what's he puttin' it on for?

DEVERY. I suppose he wants him to *keep* working for him.

BILLIE. (*After a moment.*) Too deep for *me.* (*Buzzer sounds.*)

DEVERY. (*With a step to her, lowering his voice.*) All you have to do is be nice and no rough language.

BILLIE. (*Does not like being coached. Crossing to sofa.*) I won't open my mush! (*Pronounced to rhyme with 'push.'* EDDIE *comes downstairs, goes to door.*)

DEVERY. I didn't mean that.

BILLIE. I don't have to be down here at all, y'know. I could go up-stairs. In fact I think I will. (SHE *starts out, having decided she has been insulted.*)

DEVERY. (*Intercepting her.*) I'm telling you, Billie. Harry wouldn't like it.

BILLIE. (*Making violent about face.*) All right all right all right! (SHE *moves to sofa, bristling, and sits.* EDDIE *opens door to admit* SENATOR NORVAL HEDGES *and* MRS. HEDGES. DEVERY *moves to greet them.*)

DEVERY. (*Washington joviality.*) How are you, Norval?

HEDGES. Can't complain. (*Comes down into room.*)

DEVERY. (*To* MRS. HEDGES.) Haven't seen you for a long time, Anna.

MRS. HEDGES. (*Sweetly.*) No, you haven't.

DEVERY. Come on in. (HEDGES *is a worried man of sixty. Thin, pale, and worn.* MRS. HEDGES *bears out Fanny Dixwell Holmes' comment that Washington is a city filled with great men and the women they married when they were very young. Except that the Senator is not a great man. He merely looks like a great man.*)

HEDGES. (C., *to* BILLIE.) Good evening.

BILLIE. Good evening.

DEVERY. (*Moving between* HEDGES *and* MRS. HEDGES.) Senator, you ought to remember this little lady. A great first-nighter like you. She used to be Billie Dawn?

HEDGES. (*Vaguely.*) Oh, yes — yes, indeed.

DEVERY. Billie, this is Senator Norval Hedges I've told you so much about. (HEDGES *offers his hand as* HE *crosses to her.* BILLIE *takes it.*)

HEDGES. How do you do?

BILLIE. How do you do? (HEDGES *crosses back to* C.)

DEVERY. And this is *Mrs.* Hedges, Billie.

MRS. HEDGES. (*Sitting beside* BILLIE.) Glad to meet you.

BILLIE. Glad to meet you.

DEVERY. What do you say to a drink?

MRS. HEDGES. Love one.

HEDGES. Sounds all right to me.

DEVERY. Bourbon?

HEDGES. Be fine.

DEVERY. (*To* EDDIE.) Bourbon all around, Eddie. (*Motions* HEDGES *to sit in chair* L. *of table.*)

EDDIE. Right. (HE *goes to sideboard to fix drinks.*)

HEDGES. (*Crossing to chair* L. *of table.*) That's going to hit the spot just fine. (*Sits.*)

MRS. HEDGES. (*To* BILLIE.) He's *awfully* tired.

DEVERY. (*To* HEDGES, *jocularly.*) What've you been doing? Standing over a hot resolution all day?

HEDGES. (*With a wan smile.*) Just about.

MRS. HEDGES. (*To* BILLIE.) How do you like Washington, Mrs. Brock? (DEVERY *steps quickly toward* BILLIE. *A tiny pause.* BILLIE, *turned slightly away, does not realize for an instant that she is being addressed.* DEVERY, *having taken such pains to avoid identifying her too exactly during the course of introductions, is afraid* BILLIE *may now correct* MRS. HEDGES *and ruin his careful diplomacy.* BILLIE *catches his eye.* DEVERY *nods.*)

BILLIE. Oh . . . I haven't seen it yet.

MRS. HEDGES. You mean to say this is the very first time you've been here?

BILLIE. That's what I mean. (*Grandly.*) I never went on the road.

HEDGES. Well, we must show you around. Beautiful city.

MRS. HEDGES. (*To* BILLIE.) Too bad the Supreme Court isn't in session. You'd *love* that. (*A pause.*)

BILLIE. What is it? (MRS. HEDGES *is at a loss. Looks over at* HEDGES *to see if he has any ideas.* DEVERY *saves the moment by*

27

bursting into laughter.)

DEVERY. Lots of people would like to know the answer to *that* one, Billie! (HEDGES *and* MRS. HEDGES *now settle for* BILLIE'S *remark as a piece of big-town humor which they have never been able to appreciate.* THEY *join in laughter.* EDDIE *serves* HEDGES *with drink; then* MRS. HEDGES. BILLIE *indicates to* EDDIE *that she wants a drink.* EDDIE *shakes head in refusal and crosses back to sideboard.* DEVERY *crosses to* HEDGES.) What's back of this jam Mrs. R's gotten herself into?

HEDGES. Give her enough rope. I've said so from the start.

DEVERY. I know.

HEDGES. . . . trouble with these professional do-gooders is they never seem to — (BROCK *enters from above.* HE *has changed his clothes, spruced up, wears red carnation.* HE *looks fine.*)

BROCK. (*Like a fanfare.*) Hello, everybody!

DEVERY. Here we are! (HEDGES *rises. For some reason* MRS. HEDGES *rises, too.*) Senator Hedges, Harry Brock.

BROCK. (*Heartily*) Say, it's about time us two got together, Senator. (*Shakes hands with* HEDGES, *using both hands.*)

HEDGES. About time.

BROCK. (*Crossing to* MRS. HEDGES.) And I suppose this is Mrs. Hedges?

MRS. HEDGES. That's right.

BROCK. (*Extending his hand.*) I certainly am happy to make your acquaintance. (*She takes his hand, he unbalances her with cordiality.*)

MRS. HEDGES. (*Holding her pained hand.*) Thank you so much.

BROCK. (*To* MRS. HEDGES.) Sit down. (*To* HEDGES.) Senator, sit down. (THEY *do so.* BROCK *stands* C. EDDIE *brings* BROCK *drink, then goes out.*)

HEDGES. Have a good trip down?

BROCK. Oh, sure. I come down in my car. I *came.* (*Sips his drink.*) Had to stop off in Baltimore on the way. I got a yard there, you know. A junk yard.

HEDGES. Is that so?

BROCK. Yeah. Just a *little* racket. Tell you the truth, it ain't worth the trouble it takes to run it, but I like it. It was the second yard I picked up . . . Before that I only had one yard.

MRS. HEDGES. How many do you have now?

BROCK. Hell, I don't know. (*Stops abruptly. Then blushingly apologizes to* MRS. HEDGES.) Excuse *me!*

MRS. HEDGES. (*Big about it.*) Oh, that's all right.

BROCK. (*To* HEDGES.) I don' know why I like that little Baltimore outfit. I just always get kind of a feelin' from it. Y'know what I mean?

HEDGES. Sentimental.

BROCK. That's it! I'm sentimental. Like you say.

MRS. HEDGES. I think we're *all* a bit sentimental.

BROCK. Yes. (*A pause. For some reason it seems* BILLIE'S *turn to speak.*)

BILLIE. Well —— (*All look at her. Finally.*) It's a free country! (*The company reacts variously.*)

BROCK. (*Desperately changing subject.*) How's things with you, Senator?

HEDGES. Same old grind.

BROCK. Lemme tell you sump'n, Senator. You got one job I don't never wanna be. Everybody pesterin' you all the time, prob'ly.

HEDGES. Part of the job. (BROCK *and* HEDGES *drink.*)

MRS. HEDGES. Do you play bridge, Mrs. Block? (BROCK *and* DEVERY *exchange glance* BROCK *moves to behind sofa.*)

BILLIE. No. Only Gin.

MRS. HEDGES. I beg your pardon?

BILLIE. Gin Rummy.

MRS. HEDGES. Oh, yes, of course. I was going to ask you to join us? A few of the girls? We meet now and then.

BILLIE. Yuh. Well, I don't play bridge.

BROCK. (*To* BILLIE, *hard, from behind* MRS. HEDGES.) You could learn to if you wanted!

BILLIE. (*Snapping back.*) I don't think so!

BROCK. (*Topping her.*) Sure you could! (*To* MRS. HEDGES, *suddenly and smilingly.*) She couldn't play Gin till I learned her, now she beats my brains out! (*As* MRS. HEDGES *turns back to* BILLIE, HE *gives latter a murderous look.*)

DEVERY. (*Crossing down to* HEDGES.) How're you fixed for time tomorrow, Norval?

HEDGES. Pretty tight, I'm afraid.

DEVERY. Oh. I wanted to bring Harry over on a few things.

HEDGES. Ten o'clock all right?

DEVERY. How's that for you, Harry?

BROCK. In the morning?

HEDGES. Yes.

BROCK. Pretty early for me.

BILLIE. Hah! I'll say! (BROCK's *head snaps around.*)
HEDGES. Eleven?
BROCK. Okay.
DEVERY. Where'll you be?
HEDGES. (*Awkwardly.*) Well, I can drop by here if that's all right.
DEVERY. Sure.
HEDGES. (*Lamely.*) It's right on my way. (BROCK *and* HEDGES *drink.* DEVERY *smokes.* BILLIE *rises. Pause.*)
BILLIE. (*To* MRS. HEDGES.) You wanna wash your hands or anything, honey? (HEDGES *and* BROCK *hastily drink, while* DEVERY *smokes furiously.*)
MRS. HEDGES. (*So shocked that her reply is soundless.*) No, thank you. (BILLIE *moves upstairs, languidly, through an atmosphere of tense embarrassment.* EDDIE *crosses to* BROCK, *takes his glass to sideboard, goes out.*)
DEVERY. (*To* HEDGES.) I hope you're free on Friday night?
HEDGES. I think so. (*To* MRS. HEDGES.) Are we, dear?
MRS. HEDGES. Well, we *can* be.
DEVERY. Fine.
BROCK. (*Crossing to sofa, sitting beside* MRS. HEDGES.) Atta girl!
DEVERY. . . . doing a little dinner. Few people I want Harry to meet.
HEDGES. And who want to meet *him*, I'm sure.
BROCK. (*Coyly.*) Say, listen, Senator. I'm just a junk man.
HEDGES. (*For the record.*) That's no disgrace in America.
DEVERY. (*Almost sardonic.*) No, not if you're a big junk man. (*Crosses* R. *to back of table. A pause.* BROCK *puts arm on back of sofa, almost embracing* MRS. HEDGES. *She glances at his hand behind her.*)
HEDGES. (*Rises, crosses* L. *to* BROCK. *Softly.*) I want to thank you, Mr. Brock. For everything.
BROCK. Call me Harry, Senator, willya?
HEDGES. I haven't written you about it, Harry, because—well, *you* understand. But I want you to know that I'm grateful for all you've done. For your support.
BROCK. Don't mention it. Just tit for tat. (HE *stops, confused, then turns to* MRS. HEDGES.) *Excuse me!!* (*A horrified, apologetic look at* HEDGES. HE *looks at floor, plainly ashamed of himself.*)
MRS. HEDGES. (*At sea.*) Quite all right. (DEVERY *goes to sideboard for further fortification.*)

BROCK. (*To* HEDGES.) You see, Senator, what I think is like this
—there's a certain kind of people oughta stick together.
HEDGES. My feeling. (*Returns to his chair.*)
BROCK. You know what I'm interested in. Scrap iron. I wanna buy
it—I wanna move it—and I wanna sell it. And I don't want a lot
of buttin' in with rules and regulations at no stage of the game.
HEDGES. Obviously.
BROCK. (*Rising, moving to* HEDGES.) I ain't talkin' about pea-
nuts, mind you. All this junk I been sellin' for the last fifteen
years—well, it's junk again. And I can sell it again once I lay my
hands on it. Do you know how much scrap iron is layin' around
all over Europe? Where the war was?
HEDGES. No, I don't.
BROCK. Well, I don't neither. Nobody knows. Nobody ever *will*
know. It's more than you can think of. Well, I want to pick it up
and bring it back where it belongs. Where it came from. Where I
can use it. Who does it belong to, anyways?
MRS. HEDGES. Why, isn't that interesting!
HEDGES. I have a copy for you of the preliminary survey made
by—
BROCK. (*Crossing* R. *above table, sitting chair* R. *of table.*) Boil it
down and give it to me fast. I didn't come down here to have to
do a lotta paper work. See, the way I work is this way. It's every
man for himself. Like dog eat dog. Like *you* gotta get the other
guy before he gets *you*.
HEDGES. Exactly.
BROCK. (*With relish.*) What I got in mind is an operatin' combo
—all over the world. There's enough in it for everybody—if
they're *in*, that is. Up to now, I'm doin' fine. Everybody's lined
up, everybody understands everybody. I wanna get movin', see?
—that's all. Only thing is, Ed here comes up with some new
trouble every day. *This* law, *that* law, tariffs, taxes, State Department, *this* department, *that* department—(EDDIE *comes in from
service wing, goes to sideboard.*)
DEVERY. (*Crossing to table, taking position between* BROCK *and*
HEDGES.) I'm sure you understand, Norval, that in an operation
of this kind—
BROCK. Listen, all that stuff is just a lotta hot air to me. There's
a way to do anything. That's all I know. It's up to you guys to
find out how.
DEVERY. Norval's been working along those lines.

31

HEDGES. Yes. The Hedges-Keller Amendment, for example, guarantees no interference with free enterprise—foreign or domestic. We're doing everything we can to get it through quickly.

BROCK. Well, see that you do, 'cause that's why I'm here. To see that I get what I paid for.

DEVERY. (*Picking up* HEDGES' *glass.*) One more?

HEDGES. I think not.

BROCK. (*Insisting.*) One for the road.

HEDGES. (*Giving in.*) All right. (DEVERY *gives glass to* EDDIE, *who refills it.*)

BROCK. (*Leaning back.*) How's things look to you, Senator?

HEDGES. Generally?

BROCK. Yeah, generally.

HEDGES. Well, not too bad. Just a question of staying on the alert.

BROCK. Tellin' me! (DEVERY *gets drink from* EDDIE, *brings it to table.*)

HEDGES. (*A look at* DEVERY.) I said to Sam only last week, "This country will soon have to decide if the people are going to run the Government or the Government is going to run the people."

BROCK. You said it. You know where I'd be if I had to start my business today? Up the creek! (*Again mortified, looks across to* MRS. HEDGES.) *Excuse me!!* (*This time* SHE *simply nods.*)

DEVERY. That's good sound thinking, Norval.

HEDGES. Thank you.

DEVERY. Worthy of Holmes.

HEDGES. Great man, Holmes.

DEVERY. My personal god.

BROCK. Who?

DEVERY. Oliver Wendell Holmes, Junior.

HEDGES. A wonderful man.

BROCK. Is *he* comin' Friday night? (*Awkward pause.* EDDIE *takes* MRS. HEDGES' *glass.*)

DEVERY. (*Quietly.*) I don't think so.

BROCK. Oh.

HEDGES. (*Rising.*) Well, we mustn't keep you.

MRS. HEDGES. (*Rising.*) No, we mustn't.

BROCK. (*Rising.*) Don't go. We stay up all the time.

HEDGES. Well, don't think of this as a proper visit. We just wanted to say hello. We'll be seeing a lot of each other, I'm sure. (THE HEDGES *start to go.*)

BROCK. (*Putting hand on* HEDGES' *shoulder.*) Right. Now, wait a second! (*Moves quickly to cigar box, takes out a double handful of cigars.*) Brought these down special. (*Hands them to* HEDGES.)

HEDGES. (*Taking them.*) Very kind of you. (*Moves to door.*)

BROCK. Don't mention it.

HEDGES. Good night, Harry. (BILLIE *returns.*)

BROCK. (*Patting* HEDGES *on back as they cross to door.*) Senator, it's a pleasure.

MRS. HEDGES. (*Going to door.*) Good-night, Mrs. Brock. (DEVERY *prompts* BILLIE.)

BILLIE. (*On stairs.*) Good-night.

MRS. HEDGES. Good-night and thank you so much. (SHE *starts to shake hands with* BROCK, *changes mind, withdraws hand.*)

BROCK. For what? Wait till I get settled down here. I'll show you sump'n to thank me for.

MRS. HEDGES. Good-night, Good-night, Ed. (*Gets* HEDGES' *hat.*)

DEVERY. (*Moving to door.*) See you tomorrow, Norval.

HEDGES. That's right. Good-night. (THE HEDGES *leave.* DEVERY *closes door after them.* BROCK *mops his brow, unbuttons coat.*)

BILLIE. (*Crossing to sofa.*) Good-night, all. (EDDIE *clears glasses.*)

BROCK. Okay, Eddie. Knock off.

EDDIE. Right. (HE *starts out.*)

DEVERY. Wait a minute. (EDDIE *stops.* DEVERY *goes to his briefcase, gets out some papers, which* EDDIE *signs during following scene, sitting* R. *of table.*)

BILLIE. Drips.

BROCK. What?

BILLIE. I said they're drips.

BROCK. Who the hell are you to say?

BILLIE. (*Sitting.*) I'm myself, that's who.

BROCK. Well, shut up. Nobody asked you.

BILLIE. (*Haughtily.*) Pardon me for livin'. (BROCK *crosses to chair* L. *of table, sits, takes off shoes. Looks at* DEVERY—*then, to* BILLIE.)

BROCK. Get upstairs.

BILLIE. Not yet.

BROCK. (*Rising and crossing* C. *angrily.*) Get upstairs, I told you! (*The usual tenseness between them. Finally* BILLIE *rises, goes upstairs with an air of going because she wants to. Closes her door behind her.* BROCK *moves to sofa and sits. Lights cigarette, and*

33

cogitates moodily.)

EDDIE. (*Pointing to document.*) Here, too?

DEVERY. Yes.

EDDIE. (*Looking up at* DEVERY, *offended.*) Since when I'm only the Vice-President?

DEVERY. You're slipping.

EDDIE. I used to be the *whole* President. Right?

BROCK. (*Automatically.*) That's right! (HE *comes to, shouts across to* EDDIE.) Butt out, willya?! (EDDIE *resumes signing.*) She's gonna be in the way, that dame.

DEVERY. What're you going to do about it?

BROCK. I don't know. Right now I feel like to give her the brush.

DEVERY. Pretty complicated.

BROCK. I know.

DEVERY. At the moment, she owns more of you than *you* do. On paper.

BROCK. Your idea.

DEVERY. (*Crossing to* R. *of sofa.*) Yes, and a damned good one, too. Keeps you in the clear and you know what it saves you?

BROCK. I know, I know. You told me a million times.

DEVERY. Sorry.

BROCK. You better think sump'n up. She's gonna louse me up all thé way down the line . . . God damn dumb broad!

DEVERY. Send her home.

BROCK. No.

DEVERY. Why not?

BROCK. (*Softly.*) I'm nuts about 'er. (DEVERY *looks at him quickly, in surprise.*)

DEVERY. (*Turning away, crossing* R. *to table.*) Can't have your cake and eat it.

BROCK. What?

DEVERY. Just a saying.

BROCK. It don't make sense.

DEVERY. All right. (BROCK *thinks it over. Then apparently giving up, leans back on sofa. A long pause. Suddenly straightens up.*)

BROCK. (*To* DEVERY.) What's *cakes* got to do with it?

DEVERY. Nothing, Harry. (EDDIE *finishes signing.*)

EDDIE. Okay? (DEVERY *picks up papers, looks over signatures.*)

DEVERY. Okay. (EDDIE *picks up* BROCK'S *shoes, goes upstairs to* BROCK'S *room.*)

BROCK. . . . must be a way to smarten 'er up a little. Ain't there?

DEVERY. (*Cross* U.C. *to chair with brief-case. Then* D. *to* R. *of sofa.*) I suppose so.

BROCK. Some kinda school we could send 'er to maybe?

DEVERY. I doubt that.

BROCK. Then *what?*

DEVERY. Well, we might be able to find someone who could smooth the rough edges off.

BROCK. How?

DEVERY. Let me think about it. And while I'm thinking about that, Harry, there's something you might be turning over in *your* mind.

BROCK. Yeah, what?

DEVERY. Well, if you've got to have her around you—the possibility of getting married.

BROCK. Not me.

DEVERY. Why not?

BROCK. I *been* married. I don't like it. (EDDIE *comes downstairs and goes out to service wing.*)

DEVERY. How long have you—you know—*been* with Billie?

BROCK. I don't know. Eight, nine years. Why?

DEVERY. Well, what the hell?

BROCK. It gets different when you get married.

DEVERY. Why should it?

BROCK. How do I know why should it? It just does, that's all.

DEVERY. All right. (*A pause.*)

BROCK. This way, I give her sump'n I'm a hell of a fella. We get married she's got it *comin'* she thinks.

DEVERY. (*Crossing* R. *to table.*) Billie's not like that.

BROCK. A broad's a broad.

DEVERY. Time may come you'll be sorry.

BROCK. (*Rising.*) Don't shove me.

DEVERY. All right. (*Gives* BROCK *a patronizing look. Goes up to sideboard, pours drink.*)

BROCK. (*Crossing* C. *Irritated.*) Don't make out like I'm some kinda dope. I know what I'm doin'.

DEVERY. Sure you do.

BROCK. All right. So don't make them Harvard College expressions on your face. So far *you* still work for *me.*

DEVERY. That's right, Harry.

BROCK. Okay. Just tell me what you think. If I feel like it, I'll do it. If not, no. (DEVERY *looks at* BROCK.) And don't give me them looks down your nose. (DEVERY *nods, quietly, and drinks.* BROCK

35

slumps into chair L. *of table, and sulks. Pause.* BROCK *smells his carnation, absently.*) What's so important I should get married all of a sudden?

DEVERY. (*Patiently.*) You're moving up, Harry.

BROCK. (*Turning to* DEVERY.) Huh?

DEVERY. (*Coming down to table.*) Bigger places. Bigger people. No matter what goes on underneath, these people make sure of their respectable fronts.

BROCK. The hell with 'em.

DEVERY. That's just talk. You're in the Big League now, and there are certain rules.

BROCK. Like what? Like you got to be married?

DEVERY. (*Crossing* R. *of table.*) No. Like you can't expect to just pass off a setup like this. There's such a thing as being *too* colorful. (*Sits at table across from* BROCK.)

BROCK. All right. I'll let you know. (*Rising, crossing* C., *worried.*) But if I do or if I don't, we gotta do sump'n with *her!* (*Looks upstairs.*) She just don't fit in. Do *you* think so?

DEVERY. Fit?

BROCK. Every time she opened her kisser tonight, sump'n wrong come out!

DEVERY. The hell of it is she doesn't realize.

BROCK. (*Crossing* R. *Desperately.*) Ed, couldn't you have a talk with 'er?

DEVERY. . . . take more than a talk, I'm afraid.

BROCK. Then *what?* (*Crosses* L.C. *to back of sofa, wrestling with his problem.*)

DEVERY. (*As* BROCK *crosses.*) It's a big job, Harry. It's not easy to make a person over. Maybe impossible. She has to have a great many things explained to her. I won't be around enough, and even if I were, I couldn't do it. No patience. Too old and I don't know enough myself. Not the kind of things she—(BROCK *snaps his fingers and cuts in, suddenly.*)

BROCK. Wait a minute!

DEVERY. What?

BROCK. (*Quietly, for a change.*) The guy from down the hall? (*He does not get ideas often. When he does, he thrills to the sensation.*)

DEVERY. Who?

BROCK. (*Moving* C.) The intraview guy. There's a smart little cookie.

DEVERY. Well—

36

BROCK. (*Selling it.*) Knows the town. Knows the angles. Very classy, with that bowing. (*Illustrates, in imitation of Paul's mannerism.*)

DEVERY. He could do it, probably, but he won't.

BROCK. Why not?

DEVERY. Well, he's not—

BROCK. I'll pay 'im whatever he wants.

DEVERY. I don't think so.

BROCK. Make you a bet. (*Goes to phone.*) What's his name again?

DEVERY. Wait a minute, Harry.

BROCK. (*Insistent. Picks up phone.*) What?

DEVERY. Verrall. Paul Verrall. Harry, I'm not sure —

BROCK. I like it. (*Into phone.*) Give me Verrall . . . yeah . . . Mr. Verrall.

DEVERY. (*Rising and losing his temper.*) I wish you wouldn't sail into things!

BROCK. (*In charge.*) Shutup! (DEVERY *moves to other side of room.* BROCK *speaks into phone.*) Hello, pal . . . Harry Brock... You got a minute? I wanna have a little talk. . . . Got a proposition to make you . . . What? . . . No, no. Nothin' like that. This is all right. . . . Absolutely legitimate. . . . Do that, will you? . . . Fine . . . I'll be right here. (*Hangs up, points to phone.*) I like that guy.

DEVERY. (*Coming back.*) Well enough to have him around with Billie all the time?

BROCK. Are you kiddin'? With them glasses? Listen, this is all right. I can feel it. I might even tap 'im for a little dope myself once in a while.

DEVERY. What about Billie? She may not care for the idea.

BROCK. (R. *of table.*) She'll do what I tell 'er.

DEVERY. That's not the point, Harry. People don't learn anything unless they want to.

BROCK. She knows what's good for her, she'll want to.

DEVERY. (*Resigned.*) You know best.

BROCK. Damn right. Listen, what do you think I ought to give 'im?

DEVERY. (*Sitting* L. *of table.*) Seems to me you ought to try just putting it on a friendly basis.

BROCK. (*Definitely.*) I don't believe in nothin' on no friendly basis. (*Buzzer sounds.*)

DEVERY. I know this fellow.

BROCK. (*Crossing up to door.*) I know lots of fellas. Money talks.

I don't want nobody doin' me no favors.

DEVERY. Why not talk it over with him and see what—? (BROCK *opens door.* PAUL *comes in.*)

BROCK. (*Heartily.*) Come on in, pal. Come on in.

PAUL. Thanks.

BROCK. (*Slapping* PAUL'S *shoulder.*) Have a drink.

PAUL. No, thanks. I'm just in the middle of something. (BROCK *points to* L. *end of sofa.*)

BROCK. Sit down, I wanna ask you sump'n. (PAUL *sits.*)

PAUL. Sure.

BROCK. How much you make a week?

PAUL. (*Leaning back on a sofa in imitation of* BROCK, *his arms spread wide.*) How should *I* know? What am I, an *accountant?* (BROCK *is delighted to hear himself quoted. Laughs.*)

BROCK. (*To* DEVERY.) I *love* this guy! (*To* PAUL, *as he sits beside him.*) What's your name again?

PAUL. Verrall.

BROCK. No, I mean your—uh—regular name?

PAUL. Paul.

BROCK. Listen, Paul. Here's the layout. I got a friend. Nice kid. I think you probably seen her in here before. Billie?

PAUL. Oh, yes.

BROCK. (*In confidence.*) Well, she's a good kid. Only to tell you the truth, a little on the stupid side. Not her fault, y'understand. I got 'er out of the chorus. For the chorus she was smart enough, but I'm scared she's gonna be unhappy in this town. She's never been around with such kind of people, you know what I mean?

PAUL. No.

BROCK. Well, I figure a guy like you could help her out. And me, too.

PAUL. How?

BROCK. (*Persuasively.*) Show 'er the ropes, sort of. Explain 'er what goes on and all like that. In your spare time. What do you say?

PAUL. No, I don't think I could handle it, Mr. Brock.

BROCK. Means a lot to me. I'll give you two hundred bucks a week.

PAUL. All right, I'll do it. (*All three are surprised.*)

BROCK. (*To* DEVERY.) I'm tellin' you. I *love* this guy!

PAUL. When do I start?

BROCK. Right now. Why not right now?

PAUL. Fine.

BROCK. Let me like introduce you and you take it from there.

PAUL. Good.

BROCK. (*Rises, crosses a step* U.C., *gestures derisively to* DEVERY. *Shouts up stairs.*) Billie!!

BILLIE'S VOICE. What?

BROCK. Come on down here a minute! (*To* PAUL.) She's a hell of a good kid. You'll like 'er. (BILLIE *comes out onto landing, brushing hair. She wears a resplendent negligee, which reveals and explains much. Almost anyone could succeed in it.* PAUL *rises.*)

BILLIE. (*A tone of complaint.*) I'm gettin' dressed. (*Stops as she sees* PAUL.)

BROCK. It's all right. It's all right. He's a friend of the family. (BILLIE *hesitates.*) Come on, I'm tellin' you!! (BILLIE *drops brush on ottoman, comes down.*) Honey, this is Paul Verrall.

BILLIE. Yes, I know.

BROCK. (*Propels her toward* PAUL.) He wants to talk to you.

BILLIE. What about?

BROCK. You'll find out. Sit down. (HE *seats her.*) Come on up a minute, willya, Ed?

DEVERY. Sure.

BROCK. Bring the stuff. (BROCK *looks at* PAUL, *cheers him on with a fisted gesture of confidence.* DEVERY *picks up brief-case, follows* BROCK *out of room. A long pause.* BILLIE *is seemingly disinterested and unconcerned.* PAUL *is wondering how to begin. He cannot imagine. Finally:*)

PAUL. Your—friend Mr. Brock has an idea he'd like us to spend a little time together. You and me, that is.

BILLIE. (*Without looking at him.*) You don't say.

PAUL. Yes.

BILLIE. (*Turning to* PAUL.) What're *you?* Some kind of a gigolo?

PAUL. (*Smiling.*) Not exactly.

BILLIE. (*Unsmiling.*) What's the idea?

PAUL. Nothing special. (PAUL *sits at opposite end of sofa.*) He just wants me to put you wise to a few things. Show you the ropes. Answer any questions.

BILLIE. I got no questions.

PAUL. I'll give you some.

BILLIE. (*Bored.*) Thanks.

PAUL. . . . might be fun for you, in a way. There's a lot to see down here. I'd be glad to show you around.

BILLIE. (*Looking at him.*) You know this Supreme Court?

39

PAUL. Yes.

BILLIE. I'd like to take that in.

PAUL. Sure. We're on, then?

BILLIE. (*Suspiciously.*) How do you mean?

PAUL. The arrangement.

BILLIE. I don't mind. I got nothin' much to do.

PAUL. Good.

BILLIE. (*Looking up at* BROCK'S *door.*) What's he payin' you?

PAUL. Two hundred.

BILLIE. You're a sucker. You could of got more. He's got plenty.

PAUL. I'd have done it for nothing. (BILLIE *throws him a look of rare disbelief, makes the sound of a mirthless, mocking laugh.*)

BILLIE. Hah!

PAUL. (*Protesting.*) I would.

BILLIE. Why?

PAUL. This isn't work. I like it.

BILLIE. He thinks I'm too stupid, huh?

PAUL. Why, no ——

BILLIE. He's right. I'm stupid and I like it.

PAUL. You do?

BILLIE. Sure. I'm happy. I got everything I want. Two mink coats. Everything. If there's sump'n I want, I ask. And if he *don't* come across, I don't come across. (PAUL *is startled.*) If you know what I mean.

PAUL. (*Replying swiftly.*) Yes, I do.

BILLIE. (*Practically.*) So as long as I know how to get what I want, that's all I wanna know.

PAUL. As long as you know what you want.

BILLIE. Sure. (*A pause.*) What?

PAUL. As long as you know what you want.

BILLIE. (*Annoyed.*) . . . you tryin' to mix me up?

PAUL. No.

BILLIE. (*Rising, crossing* R. *to chair* L. *of table.*) I tell you what I *would* like.

PAUL. Yes?

BILLIE. (*Back of chair* L. *of table.*) I'd like to learn how to talk good.

PAUL. All right.

BILLIE. (*Turning to him.*) Is it hard to learn?

PAUL. I don't think so.

BILLIE. What do I have to do?

PAUL. Well, I might give you a few books to start with. Then, if you don't mind, I'll correct you now and then.
BILLIE. (*Crossing back to sofa.*) Go ahead.
PAUL. When I know, that is. I don't—talk so good myself.
BILLIE. You'll do.
PAUL. Fine. (*We sense that she is warming to him.*)
BILLIE. (*Sitting.*) I never say "ain't." Did you notice that? Never.
PAUL. I do.
BILLIE. Well, I'll correct *you*, then.
PAUL. Do that.
BILLIE. Since I was very small I never say it. We had this teacher. She used to slug you if you did it.
PAUL. Did what?
BILLIE. Said "ain't."
PAUL. Oh.
BILLIE. So I got outa the habit.
PAUL. You think it was worth the slugging?
BILLIE. Well, not hard.
PAUL. It's the principle of the thing. There's too much slugging. I don't believe in it.
BILLIE. (*Aping his seriousness.*) All right, I don't believe in it, either.
PAUL. Good.
BILLIE. (*Softly, leaning toward him with a smile.*) I learn pretty fast, don't I?
PAUL. (*Smiling.*) You're great, Miss Dawn.
BILLIE. (*Correcting him.*) Billie.
PAUL. Billie. (*A tiny pause.*) Sort of an odd name, isn't it?
BILLIE. (*Surprised.*) What're you talkin'? Half the kids I know are named it. Anyway, it's not my real name.
PAUL. What is?
BILLIE. (*Has to think a moment before she can answer.*) My God! —Emma.
PAUL. What's the matter?
BILLIE. Do I look to you like an Emma?
PAUL. No. You don't look like a Billie, either.
BILLIE. So what do I look like?
PAUL. To me?
BILLIE. Yuh, to you.
PAUL. You look like a little angel. (*A pause.*)
BILLIE. Lemme ask you—(*Looks at* BROCK'S *door, then leans to-*

41

ward PAUL.) Are you one of these *talkers*, or would you be inna-
rested in a little *action?*
PAUL. (*Amazed.*) Huh?
BILLIE. I got a yen for you right off.
PAUL. Do you get many?
BILLIE. Now and then.
PAUL. What do you do about them?
BILLIE. (*Invitingly.*) Stick around. You'll find out.
PAUL. All right, I will.
BILLIE. And if you want a tip, I'll tell you. Sweet talk me. I like it.
Like that angel line. (PAUL *looks upstairs, rises.*) Don't worry
about *him.* He don't see a thing. He's too dizzy from bein' a big
man.
PAUL. (*Crossing* L. *to back of sofa.*) This is going to be a little
different than I thought.
BILLIE. (*Leaning back.*) You mind?
PAUL. (*Hands on back of sofa, bends to her. His tie hangs down.*)
No.
BILLIE. (*Playing with his tie.*) It's only fair. We'll educate each
other. (PAUL *straightens up, walks* R. *around sofa.* BILLIE *sits up,
faces him.*)
PAUL. (*Weakly attempting to get on safer ground.*) Now, about
those books.
BILLIE. Yes?
PAUL. I'll get them for you tomorrow. I'll look around my place,
too. If there's anything interesting, I'll drop it by later.
BILLIE. All right.
PAUL. We can figure out time every day the day before.
BILLIE. (*Beckons to* HIM. HE *bends over, but not far enough.* SHE
hooks her finger into his breast pocket, draws him closer.) Or the
night!
PAUL. Sure. (BROCK *and* DEVERY *appear.* PAUL *and* BILLIE *separate
quickly.* BROCK *wears a foulard lounging jacket.*)
BROCK. Well. You two gonna get together?
PAUL. (*Looking at* BILLIE.) I think we're all set.
BROCK. Great! Great! (DEVERY *picks up his hat.*)
PAUL. (*Starting out.*) Well, if you'll excuse me ——
BROCK. Have a drink.
PAUL. No, thanks.
DEVERY. (*Leaving.*) See you tomorrow, Harry.
BROCK. Right.

DEVERY. Good-night, Billie.

BILLIE. So long. (DEVERY *leaves, closing door.*)

PAUL. (*To* BILLIE.) Good-night.

BROCK. (*Following* PAUL. *On second step* C. THEY *shake hands.*)
So long, kid. Appreciate it.

PAUL. (*Still shaking hands. A look at* BILLIE.) So do I.

BILLIE. (*Tantalizingly.*) So long, kid! (PAUL *leaves.* BROCK *comes
back into room, standing below stairs. Alone now for the first time
in the play, it is obvious that they have nothing whatever to say to
one another. However, there are ways and ways of social inter-
course. We are about to see one of the most common.* BROCK *takes
a Gin Rummy kit* [*two decks of cards—pencil—score pad*] *from
pocket of his robe, goes into action.* HE *moves to table* R., *puts
down cards.* BILLIE *takes cigarettes, comes over to table, cuts cards.*
HE *cuts,* THEY *compare.* SHE *slams hers down.* HE *does same.* BROCK
puts phone on floor, sits R. *of table. Shuffles, then deals two hands
of Gin Rummy.* BILLIE *goes to mix drinks, comes back to table, sets
them down.* BROCK, *arranging his hand, draws cards to his breast
with a jerk, with the alertness of one who has been bitten and is
twice shy.* BILLIE *sits, tears out top page of score pad, drops it in
ashtray.* SHE *pushes her bracelet up on her arm and straightens her
hair.* SHE *begins to sort her cards. You get the idea that this is their
nightly routine.* BROCK *downs his drink, a straight shot of rye.*
BILLIE *arranges her cards swiftly and at length, giving the unmis-
takable impression of many sets, a fine hand.* BROCK *watches her
with something less than patience. Finally, when* SHE *is ready,
game begins.* THEY *play swiftly, professionally, with no sense of
enjoyment.* SHE *discards.* BROCK *cannot use it, picks one from deck.*
HE *looks at it, discards it.* BILLIE *scoops it up.* SHE *discards, then
rearranges her hand, having obviously completed a run.* BROCK
notes this, unhappily, picks another card from deck, puts it down.
BILLIE *again scoops his discard.* SHE *moves two cards over to it,
completing another run, then discards.* BROCK, *simmering, picks
up another card from deck. His inefficient poker face breaks into a
smile as he finds he can use it.* HE *discards.* BILLIE, *as though it
were coming to her, picks it up and after a pause, during which
SHE sits motionless, discards.* BROCK *starts to draw.*)

BILLIE. (*A high note.*) Gin! (BROCK *pulls back his hand quickly.*
SHE *lays out her hand.* BROCK *scores his.*)

BROCK. (*Mumbling.*) Forty-one. (BILLIE *shoves cards to* BROCK,
picks up pencil, ready to score.)

43

BILLIE. (*Quietly.*) Forty-one?

BROCK. (*Louder.*) Forty-one! (SHE *marks score, then takes a sip of her drink.* HE *shuffles, cuts, hands her the pack.* HE *takes cigarette, lights it.* SHE *deals slowly, moving her lips as she counts inaudibly.* THEY *pick up their cards and play.* BROCK *discards first.* BILLIE *draws, discards.* BROCK *draws again.*) If you pay attention, that Verrall guy can do you some good.

BILLIE. (*Not looking up.*) All right. (*Draws and discards.*)

BROCK. (*Draws.*) You're in the Big League now. I want you to watch your step. (*Discards.*)

BILLIE. (*Still absorbed in game.*) All right. (*Draws and discards.* BROCK *draws and discards.*)

BROCK. You gotta learn to fit in. If not, I can't have you around, and that's no bull. (*A pause, as* THEY *play.* BILLIE *draws and discards.*) You gotta be careful what you *do.* (*Draws and discards.*) And what you *say!*

BILLIE. (*Picking up his discard.*) Three! (*Lays out her hand.*)

BROCK. (*Scores his cards. Lays one off on her hand.*) Twenty-eight.

BILLIE. (*Pencil poised, ready to score.* SHE *wants to hear him say it again.*) Twenty-eight?

BROCK. (*Too clearly.*) Twenty-eight! (BILLIE *shoves cards to* BROCK *for him to shuffle.* SHE *starts to score. Arithmetic is not her strong point, so using her* L. *hand, on which* SHE *is resting her head,* SHE *counts with her fingers, tapping them in sequence against her forehead. In this way,* SHE *achieves total, scores it, then leans back.*)

BILLIE. You could use a little education yourself, if you ask me.

BROCK. Who asked you?

BILLIE. Nobody.

BROCK. So shut up! (*Hands cards over.* BILLIE *deals, her annoyance speeding tempo, and again counting inaudibly. When she has finished, she slams down remainder of deck.*)

BILLIE. Can't I talk?

BROCK. Play your cards. (*Pause.* SHE *begins to sort cards.*)

BILLIE. (*Loudly.*) It's a free country.

BROCK. (*Discards.*) That's what *you* think. (*A pause.* BILLIE *starts to sing "Anything Goes," without words. Her memory of the song includes the orchestration, complete with breaks, trumpet figures and percussion.* SHE *gets through sixteen bars,* BROCK *becoming increasingly annoyed.* HE *has picked up a card, but her singing has so disconcerted him that* HE *cannot make a decision.*)

44

BILLIE. (*Imitating muted trumpet.*) Tyah—dah—!
BROCK. (*Yelling.*) Do you mind? (*Looks first at his card, then at his hand, discards.*)
BILLIE. (*Picking up his discard.*) Gin. (SHE *lays out her hand, as* BROCK *begins to resemble the King of Diamonds.*)
BROCK. (*Scores his cards.*) Thirty-four.
BILLIE. (*Ready with pencil as before.*) Thirty-four?
BROCK. Thirty-four!
BILLIE. (*Scores, as before, as* HE *shuffles, then with a smile and a shout.*) Schneider!
BROCK. (*Stops shuffling.*) Where do you get the schneid? (BILLIE *twists score-pad around to prove it.*)
BILLIE. Fifty-five dollars. And sixty cents.
BROCK. (*Petulantly.*) All right, that's all! (BROCK *throws down cards, rises. Crosses to sideboard, pours drink.*)
BILLIE. Pay me now.
BROCK. (*Yelling.*) What the hell's the matter? Don't you trust me?
BILLIE. What are you hollerin'? You always make *me* pay.
BROCK. (*Annoyed.*) Christ sake!
BILLIE. (*Taunting him in sing-song.*) Sore loser!
BROCK. Shut up!
BILLIE. (*With perfect, ladylike control.*) Fifty-five dollars and sixty cents. (HE *comes down to table, takes large roll of bills from his pocket, pays off fifty-five dollars.* HE *starts to go, but* BILLIE *stops him with a querying look. Pained, but resigned to defeat,* HE *counts out change, two quarters and a dime, tosses them to her across table.* SHE *slaps each one into possession.*) Thanks. (HE *starts for staircase, stops directly behind* BILLIE, *looks down at her with predatory eyes.*)
BROCK. Come on up.
BILLIE. (*Casually.*) In a minute. (BROCK *starts up stairs.*)
BROCK. (*Stops on second step.*) Now! (*This is the one moment in their daily life of which Billie is boss.* BOTH *recognize the fact.*)
BILLIE. (*In charge.*) In a minute, I told you! (SHE *riffles cards.* BROCK *goes up quietly, shuts door.* BILLIE *moves her winnings to one side, clears table in front of her and lays out a hand of solitaire. She sings, softly, as before, and plays in time to music. This time we hear the lyrics, as they were carefully coached into the chorus.*)
         "In olden days a glimpse of stocking
         Was looked on as something shocking

But now Lord knows (tyah dah)
Anything Goes (tata tata—tata tata—tzing!)
Good authors, too, who once—"
(*Door buzzer sounds.* SHE *stops singing, looks upstairs, makes a few personal adjustments, goes to door and opens it.* PAUL *comes in, carrying a few books and two newspapers.*)
PAUL. Hello.
BILLIE. (*Feigning surprise.*) Hello!
PAUL. Morning papers. (*Offers them to her.*)
BILLIE. You could of saved yourself the trouble. I don't read papers.
PAUL. Never?
BILLIE. Once in a while the back part.
PAUL. I think you should. The front part.
BILLIE. Why?
PAUL. It's interesting.
BILLIE. Not to me.
PAUL. How do you know if you never read it?
BILLIE. Look, if you're gonna turn out to be a pest, we could call the whole thing off right now.
PAUL. Sorry.
BILLIE. I look at the paper sometimes. I just never understand it. So what's the sense?
PAUL. Tell you what you do. You look through these. (HE *gives her newspapers.*) Anything you don't understand, make a mark. (*Takes red editing pencil from his pocket and hands it to her.*) Then, tomorrow, I'll explain whatever I can. All right?
BILLIE. All right.
PAUL. (*Adding books.*) And I thought you might like these.
BILLIE. I'll try. (SHE *puts books and newspapers on top of book-case.*)
PAUL. No, don't do that. Just start reading. If you don't like it, stop. Start something else.
BILLIE. (*Coming back to him.*) There's only one thing. My eyesight isn't so hot.
PAUL. Well, why don't you wear glasses?
BILLIE. (*Aghast.*) Glasses!
PAUL. Why not?
BILLIE. Because they're terrible! (THEY *look at each other for a time.* SHE *notices his glasses, but cannot think of anything to say that will soften her remark.* SHE *moves in closer to him. Then*

46

closer still. It is as though they were about to dance. SHE *leans toward him.* Now THEY *are touching. All at once* THEY *melt into an embrace, and kiss. A long expert kiss.* THEY *come out of it.* BILLIE *continues, casually.*) Of course, they're not so bad on men.

PAUL. (*Softly.*) Good-night, Billie.

BILLIE. Good-night. (PAUL *leaves,* BILLIE *looks after him, then with a new smile* SHE *starts to sing. In time to music, moves to light switch* R. *of door.*)

"Good authors, too, who once knew better words—"

(*Snaps out sitting-room lights. Balcony is still illuminated. Starts up stairs, slowly, continuing song.*)

"Now only use four-letter words
Writing prose (tyah dah)—"

(SHE *stops, pivots on last phrase, then moves down stairs, picks up newspapers and books, clutches them tightly, starts up again, singing.*)

"Writing prose—"

(SHE *reaches top of stairs, sings the break through* HARRY'S *closed door as two notes of derision.*)

"Tyah! Dah!"

(SHE *enters her own room as she finishes the phrase triumphantly.*)
"Anything goes!"

(SHE *slams the door closed. The room is in darkness.*)

FAST CURTAIN

ACT II

SCENE: *The same. About two months have passed. The room looks liveu in. A desk has replaced table R.C. It is loaded with books, papers, copies of The New Republic, clippings, tall glass filled with pencils, phone, memo pad, desk basket. On down stage chair R. are record albums and a large paper map. In front of this chair is a large globe map on a pedestal. The shelves of the sideboard are filled with books. Also books on floor under sideboard. On chair L. and downstage of sideboard is a large framed Picasso reproduction. On floor under chair a pile of art folios. In front of balcony are four piles*

47

of books, mostly new. Large ottoman on balcony holds map and more pictures. On either side of main door hangs a small framed John Whorf watercolor. On chair R. of main doors are some envelopes, including a large brown one, containing legal papers. Shelves back of sofa are filled with books and there are stacks of them on top of bookcases. Also on bookcase is a silver tray with liquor, ginger ale, glasses, water and ice-bucket. On top of small table L. is a stack of newspapers and magazines, such as Harper's, Atlantic Monthly, Kenyon Review, etc. On floor and step near window L. are strewn more magazines. Down L. is a huge unabridged dictionary on its stand. On shelf of this stand is a pile of New York Times and Herald-Tribune Sunday book review sections, and on floor under shelf are magazines and books. In addition to cig-arette box and ashtray on top of end table L. of sofa, is a copy of "David Copperfield" with a book-mark in it, a pile of three books, a brandy snifter containing pencils, including several red editing ones and a small pad. On sofa is a copy of The New York Times and one of The Washington Post. A silver service with remains of tea and cookies is on coffee table front of sofa and under tray is a black memo book [containing a pencil] and a letter addressed to "Miss Billie Dawn". There is a copy of Flair on chair L. of desk and other magazines on floor. In front of fireplace R. is a Capehart, with many record albums on floor leaning against it. In record rack on upstage end of Capehart are three large Red Seal records and some smaller ones.

AT RISE: *It is early evening and* BILLIE, *wearing slacks, blouse, robe and eyeglasses, is sitting on sofa reading front page of Washington Post. She opens paper and lifts it high to continue her reading. Front page of paper is covered with red marks. It is as though this newspaper has the measles. She puts paper down and stretches, takes off glasses and puts them on coffee table, then gets up and walks across room to Capehart.* SHE *limps in an odd way, indicating that her leg has gone to sleep. At Capehart she selects three large records from record rack, holding them, one by one, close to her eyes in an effort to make out titles. Her nose touches record each time. She places records in instrument, starts it and walks back across room as music starts to play softly. The recording is of*

Jascha Heifetz playing the andante movement of the Concerto in D Minor for Violin and Orchestra, Op. 47, by Jan Sibelius. She sits, puts on glasses again, picks up newspaper, starts to read. Before long she comes across a point she does not understand. She takes red pencil from glass and begins to mark paper. Buzzer sounds. EDDIE *comes into room from service wing, wearing his hat, as always. As he enters, he sees* BILLIE *marking paper. Shakes head sympathetically and continues to door, opening it to admit* PAUL. *At sound of his voice,* BILLIE *smiles, puts down paper, whips off glasses and puts them on end table.*

PAUL. How are you, Eddie?
EDDIE. Great.
PAUL. (*To* BILLIE.) Hello, smarty-pants. (EDDIE *returns to service wing.*)
BILLIE. Hello.
PAUL. (*Moving to her.*) How you coming?
BILLIE. Not so bad.
PAUL. (*Teacher to pupil.*) Hm?
BILLIE. —ly. Bad*ly.* (PAUL *laughs.*) Would you like some tea?
PAUL. (*Sitting on sofa.*) No thanks. (*Listens to music.*) Nice, that.
BILLIE. Sibelius, *opp* Forty-seven. (*She pronounces it 'Sy-beel-ious.'* THEY *listen together for a moment.*) Guess who I just had for tea? *To* tea?
PAUL. Who?
BILLIE. (*Impressively.*) Mrs. Hedges.
PAUL. Really? How was it?
BILLIE. Don't ask! You know, she's pretty stupid, too—but in a refined sort of a way. Of course, we didn't have very much to talk about—so then she happened to notice my book laying there ——
PAUL. Lying.
BILLIE. —my book *lying* there, and she says, "Oh, I've been meaning to read that again for years!"
PAUL. What was it?
BILLIE. (*Matter-of-fact.*) *David Copperfield.*
PAUL. Oh yes.
BILLIE. So then we got to talking about it, and you want to know something?
PAUL. What?

49

BILLIE. (*Telling a secret.*) She's never read it at *all!*
PAUL. How do you know?
BILLIE. I could tell from the way we were talking.
PAUL. . . . . that surprise you?
BILLIE. What, that she never read it?
PAUL. Yes.
BILLIE. No.
PAUL. Then what?
BILLIE. Well, why should she make out like she did? It's no crime if she didn't.
PAUL. Everybody does that, more or less.
BILLIE. Do you?
PAUL. Sometimes.
BILLIE. *I* don't.
PAUL. I know, Billie. You're an honest one.
BILLIE. Thanks. I'm glad I got something from two months of this. (WAITER *enters from service wing, crosses to coffee table. Picks up tray, revealing letter which lies under it.*)
PAUL. You didn't get that from me, I'm afraid. (WAITER *starts to go.*)
BILLIE. I'm not so sure.
PAUL. (*Prompting.*) Thank you.
BILLIE. (*Pleasantly.*) You're welcome.
PAUL. (*Indicating* WAITER.) No, no.
BILLIE. Oh —— (*Calling to* WAITER.) Thank you! (WAITER *turns, bows, leaves.* BILLIE *picks up letter from coffee table, looks at it.*) I got this letter today. From my father.
PAUL. New York?
BILLIE. Yuh. I can't get over it.
PAUL. Why?
BILLIE. Well, it's the first time he ever wrote me in about eight years. We had a fight, sort of. He didn't want me to go with Harry.
PAUL. What does he do?
BILLIE. My father?
PAUL. Yes.
BILLIE. Gas Company. He used to read meters, but in this letter he says how he can't get around so good any more so they gave him a different job. Elevator man. (*A pause, as she remembers back. Music is still playing. She continues with a little smile of instinctive affection.*) Goofy old guy. He used to take a little frying pan to work every morning and a can of Sterno and cook his own

lunch. He said everybody should have a hot lunch. (*Another pause.*) I swear I don't know how he did it. There were four of us. Me and my three brothers and he had to do everything. My mother died. I never knew her. He used to feed us and give us a bath —— buy our clothes. Everything. That's why all my life I used to think how some day I'd like to pay him back. Funny how it worked out. One night, I brought home a hundred dollars and I gave it to him. You know what he did? He threw it in the toilet and pulled the chain. I thought he was going to hit me, sure, but he didn't. In his whole life, he never hit me once.

PAUL. (*Carefully.*) How'd he happen to write you? I mean, after all this time?

BILLIE. Because I wrote *him.*

PAUL. Oh.

BILLIE. He says he's thought about me every day. God. I haven't thought about him, I bet, once even, in five years. That's nothin' against him. I haven't thought of anything.

PAUL. . . . nice to see him, maybe.

BILLIE. I guess so—but he says I should write him again and I should have a hot lunch everyday and I should let him know how I am but that he didn't want to see me if I was still living the life of a concubine . . . I looked it up! . . . He always used to say: "Don't ever do nothin' you wouldn't want printed on the front page of the New York Times." (*A pause.*) Hey! I just realized I've practically told you the whole story of my life by now practically. (*Puts letter back on coffee table.*)

PAUL. . . . enjoyed it very much.

BILLIE. (*Settling back.*) How about the story of *your* life?

PAUL. Oh no. It's too long —— and mostly untrue. (THEY *smile at each other.*) What'd you do this morning?

BILLIE. (*Brightening*) Oh, I went to the newsreel and then over to the National Gallery like you said. (SHE *rises. Takes letter from coffee table, crosses* R. *to desk.*)

PAUL. How was it?

BILLIE. Wonderful. Quiet and peaceful and so interesting and did you ever notice? It *smells* nice. (PAUL *smiles.*) It *does.*

PAUL. How long'd you stay?

BILLIE. (*Putting letter in desk drawer.*) Couple hours. I'm goin' again.

PAUL. Good.

BILLIE. Only the next time I wish you could come along.

51

PAUL. All right.

BILLIE. (*Crossing* C.) Boy, there's sure some things *there* that could use some explaining. (*Sibelius music ends. A moment of silence, then the lovely strains of "On Hearing The First Cuckoo of Spring," by Dēlius, are heard.*) Oh, and you know what else I did today? I went down to Brentano's and I just walked around, like you said I should, and I looked at all the different kinds of books, and then the ones I thought maybe I'd like to read I took.

PAUL. That's right.

BILLIE. Well, so pretty soon I had a whole big pile, too big to carry, even. So I stopped. And I thought, my God, it'll take me about a year to read this many! So then I looked around, and compared to all the books there, my little pile was like nothing. So then I realized that even if I read my eyes out till the day I die I couldn't even make a little dent in that *one store*. Next thing you know I bust out cryin'. (*Crosses* L. *behind couch.*)

PAUL. (*Rising, crossing* R. *to desk.*) Nobody reads everything.

BILLIE. They don't?

PAUL. Of course not.

BILLIE. (*Moving around to front of sofa and sitting.*) I sure been tryin' to.

PAUL. (*Looking through a copy of New Republic.*) . . . don't suppose you got a chance to read my piece?

BILLIE. What're you talkin'? Of course I did. *Twice.* (*A pause.*)

PAUL. What'd you think?

BILLIE. (*Slowly and deliberately.*) Well, I think it's the best thing I ever read. I didn't understand *one word!* (PAUL *turns to place and looks at it.*)

PAUL. What didn't you understand?

BILLIE. None of it.

PAUL. (*Beckoning* BILLIE *to desk; holding copy out to her.*) Here, show me what. (BILLIE *rises, puts on glasses as she goes to desk.* PAUL *laughs.* SHE *stops.*)

BILLIE. What's so funny? That I'm blind practically?

PAUL. Practically blind.

BILLIE. (*Continuing to desk.*) —— practically blind?

PAUL. You're wonderful.

BILLIE. (*At desk, stiffly.*) I'm sorry I look funny to you.

PAUL. You don't. They make you look lovelier than ever.

BILLIE. (*Sitting at desk.*) You sound like one of them ads for eye-glasses. (SHE *puts her attention on article.* PAUL *comes to*

52

her.)

PAUL. (*Putting magazine in front of her.*) What?

BILLIE. Well, like the name of it. "The Yellowing Democratic Manifesto."

PAUL. Simple.

BILLIE. To who? Whom. Whom? Well, anyway, not to me.

PAUL. Well, look. You know what 'yellowing' means?

BILLIE. Not this time.

PAUL. (*Trying to explain.*) When a piece of paper gets old, what happens to it? (BILLIE *thinks.*)

BILLIE. Throw it away?

PAUL. No, it turns yellow.

BILLIE. It does?

PAUL. Of course.

BILLIE. What do you know!

PAUL. Now, 'democratic'. You know what *that* means, don't you?

BILLIE. (*Nodding.*) Not Republican.

PAUL. Well, not exactly. It just means pertaining to our form of Government, which is a democracy.

BILLIE. (*Understanding.*) Oh. (*A pause.*) What's 'pertaining'?

PAUL. (*With a descriptive gesture.*) Has to do with.

BILLIE. (*Musing.*) 'Pertaining'. Nice word. (*Writes it down.*)

PAUL. All right, now — 'manifesto' ?

BILLIE. I don't know.

PAUL. Why didn't you look it up?

BILLIE. I *did* look it up. I *still* don't know.

PAUL. Well, look —— when I say 'manifesto', I mean the set of rules and ideals and —— principles and hopes on which the United States is based.

BILLIE. And you think it's turning yellow?

PAUL. Well, yes. I think that a lot of the original inspiration's been neglected—and forgotten.

BILLIE. And that's bad?

PAUL. And that's bad. (SHE *thinks it over for a moment, hard. We can almost see it soaking in.* SHE *looks at magazine again.*)

BILLIE. (*Reading.*) "Even a . . . cursory? . . . (*Looks up at* PAUL, *who nods.*) examination of contemporary society in terms of the Greek philosophy which defines the whole as a representation— of its parts, sends one immediately—to the consideration of the individual—as a citizen and the citizen as an individual."

PAUL. Well —— ?

53

BILLIE. (*Exasperated.*) I looked up every word!

PAUL. (*Closer to her.*) Listen—thousands of years ago, a Greek philosopher — (HE *pauses to make sure she is following.*) —said that the world could only be as good as the people who lived in it. (BILLIE *thinks this over.*)

BILLIE. (*Generously.*) Makes sense.

PAUL. All right. So I said, you take one look at America today and right away you figure you better take a look at the people *in* it. One by one, sort of.

BILLIE. Yuh . . . ?

PAUL. That's all.

BILLIE. (*Pointing to article.*) That's this?

PAUL. Sure.

BILLIE. Well, why didn't you say so?

PAUL. (*Crossing behind desk to* C.) Too fancy, huh? (HE *turns to her.*) I better do that piece again. Plainer. (HE *sits on* R. *arm of sofa. The music changes to a violin recording of "The Maid With The Flaxen Hair" by Debussy.*)

BILLIE. Oh, and you know that thing you gave me about Napoleon?

PAUL. No, what?

BILLIE. By Robert G. Ingersoll?

PAUL. Oh, yes.

BILLIE. Well, I'm not sure if I get that either.

PAUL. No deep meaning there.

BILLIE. There must be. He says about how he goes and looks in Napoleon's tomb. . . .

PAUL. Yuh.

BILLIE. And he thinks of Napoleon's whole sad life. . . .

PAUL. Yuh.

BILLIE. And then in the end he says he himself would've rather been a happy farmer.

PAUL. (*Quoting softly.*) "—and I said I would rather have been a French peasant and worn wooden shoes. I would rather have lived in a hut with a vine growing over the door, and the grapes growing purple in the kisses of the autumn sun." (*Continuing, rises and crosses* D.C *to* R. *of desk.*) "I would rather have been that poor peasant with my loving wife by my side, knitting as the day died out of the sky —— with my children upon my knee and their arms about me —— I would rather have been that man and gone down to the tongueless silence of the dreamless

54

dust, than to have been that imperial impersonation of force and murder, known as Napoleon the Great'."

BILLIE. (*Awed.*) How can you remember all that stuff? (*As* PAUL *starts to sit* R. *of desk,* HE *is startled, and so is* BILLIE, *by a burst from the Capehart. Debussy has been followed by the hysterical opening of* T. *Dorsey's recording of "Well, Get It!" It rides.* BILLIE *rushes over and turns it off.* SHE *crosses back to desk, glancing at* PAUL *in apologetic embarrassment.*) Once in a while. Just for a change!

PAUL. (*Laughing.*) Don't try so hard, Billie. Please. You miss the whole point.

BILLIE. Well, I like to like what's better to like.

PAUL. There's room for all sorts of things in you. The idea of learning is to be bigger, not smaller.

BILLIE. (*Seriously.*) You think I'm gettin' bigger?

PAUL. Certainly.

BILLIE. Glad to hear it. (*Sits at desk and picks up the thread of their talk.*) So he would rather been a happy peasant than to be Napoleon. So who wouldn't?

PAUL. So Harry wouldn't, for one.

BILLIE. What makes you think not?

PAUL. Ask him.

BILLIE. (*A shrug.*) He probably never heard of Napoleon.

PAUL. What's worse, he probably never heard of a peasant.

BILLIE. You hate him like poison?

PAUL. Who, Harry?

BILLIE. Yuh.

PAUL. No.

BILLIE. But you don't like him?

PAUL. No. (*Rises and crosses* C., *below desk.*)

BILLIE. Account of me and him?

PAUL. One reason. There are lots more.

BILLIE. What?

PAUL. (C., *turning to her.*) Think about it. You'll see that Harry is a menace.

BILLIE. He's not so bad. I've seen worse.

PAUL. (*A step* R.C.) Has he ever done anything for anyone, except himself?

BILLIE. Me.

PAUL. What?

BILLIE. Well, I got two mink coats.

55

PAUL. That was a trade. You gave him something, too. (*An awkward pause before* BILLIE *replies, very quietly.*)
BILLIE. (*With rare dignity.*) Don't get dirty you're supposed to be so wonderful so don't get dirty!
PAUL. Has he ever thought about anybody but himself?
BILLIE. Who does?
PAUL. (*With increasing fervor and volume, crossing to her.*) Millions of people, Billie. The whole damned history of the world is a story of the struggle between the selfish and the unselfish!
BILLIE. (*Quietly.*) I can hear you.
PAUL. (*Patiently.*) All the bad around us is bred by selfishness. Sometimes selfishness even gets to be a cause, an organized force, even a government. Then it's called Fascism. Can you understand that?
BILLIE. Sort of.
PAUL. (*Hammering.*) Well, *think* about it, Billie.
BILLIE. (*Softly, watching him.*) You're crazy about me, aren't you?
PAUL. (*Frankly.*) Yes.
BILLIE. That's why you get so mad at Harry.
PAUL. Listen, I hate his life, what he does, what he stands for. Not him. He just doesn't know any better. (*Turns and crosses* L. *to front of couch.*)
BILLIE. (*Taking off glasses.*) I go for you, too.
PAUL. (*Turns to her.*) I'm glad of that.
BILLIE. That's why I started doin' all this. I guess you know.
PAUL. No, I didn't.
BILLIE. . . . lot of good it did me. I never had this kind of trouble before, I can tell you.
PAUL. Trouble?
BILLIE. After that first night when I met you I figured it was all going to work dandy. (PAUL *is looking at her.*) Then, when you wouldn't step across the line —— I figured maybe the way to *you* was through your —— head.
PAUL. (*Very slowly, crossing behind* HER *to* R. *of desk.*) Well—— no.
BILLIE. Anyway what's the diff now? Difference! But I like you anyways. Too late for the rest.
PAUL. Why?
BILLIE. Why? Look, Paul, there's a certain time between a fella and a girl when it either comes off or not and if it doesn't then, then it never does.

PAUL. (*Moving to her.*) Maybe we haven't got to our time yet?
BILLIE. We did, too. And you dropped the ball.
PAUL. Don't be so sure.
BILLIE. I *know*. I've had lots of fellas and I *haven't* had lots of fellas. If you know what I mean.
PAUL. Yes.
BILLIE. (*Rising, crossing* L.C.) But I sure never thought I'd go through a thing like *this* for anybody!
PAUL. Like what?
BILLIE. Like gettin' all mixed up in my head. Wondering and worrying and *thinking*—stuff like that. You know last night I went to bed and I started in thinking and I couldn't get to sleep for *ten minutes!* . . . and I don't know if it's good to find out so much so quick! (*Crosses* L. *to sofa and sits.*)
PAUL. (*Crossing* L. *to her.*) What the hell, Billie! Nobody's *born* smart. You know what's the stupidest thing on earth? An infant.
BILLIE. What've you got against babies all of a sudden?
PAUL. Nothing. I've got nothing against a brain three weeks old and empty. But when it hangs around for thirty years without absorbing anything, I began to think something's the matter with it.
BILLIE. (*Rising, deeply offended.*) What makes you think I'm thirty?
PAUL. (*Retreating.*) I didn't mean you, especially.
BILLIE. (*Crossing* L. *and around back of sofa, angrily.*) Oh yes, you did.
PAUL. I swear.
BILLIE. You certainly know how to get me sore.
PAUL. (*Crossing up to* U.R. *corner of sofa.*) I'm sorry.
BILLIE. (*Crossing to him, boiling.*) Thirty! Do I look *thirty* to you?
PAUL. No.
BILLIE. (*Face to face.*) Then what'd you say it for?
PAUL. I don't know. (*A short pause.*) How old *are* you?
BILLIE. Twenty-nine! (*They look at each other.* PAUL *smiles.* SHE *responds, reluctantly.* HE *bends down, kisses her cheek.*)
PAUL. Don't stop. (SHE *moves into an embrace.*) I meant, don't stop studying.
BILLIE. Oh. (*Crosses* L. *back of sofa to* D.L.*)*
PAUL. Will you?
BILLIE. (*Crossing* D.L. *around front of sofa.*) I don't know why it's so important to you.
PAUL. . . . sort of a cause. I want everybody to be smart. As smart

57

as they *can* be. A world full of ignorant people is too dangerous to live in.

BILLIE. (*Sitting.*) I know, that's why I wish I was doin' better.

PAUL. You're doing wonderfully.

BILLIE. Yeah, but it's just no use. I bet most people would laugh at me if they knew what I was tryin' to.

PAUL. I'm not laughing.

BILLIE. I am. I'm sort of laughin' at myself. (*Her throat clenches.*) Who do I think I *am* anyway?

PAUL. What's the matter?

BILLIE. (*In tears.*) All them books!

PAUL. (*Crossing* L. *to sofa, sitting beside* HER.) It isn't only books, Billie. I've told you a hundred times.

BILLIE. It's mostly.

PAUL. Not at all. Listen, who said this? "The proper study of mankind is man ."

BILLIE. (*Gaining control.*) I don't know.

PAUL. You should.

BILLIE. Why?

PAUL. I've told you.

BILLIE. I forgot.

PAUL. Pope.

BILLIE. The Pope?

PAUL. No, not *the* Pope. *Alexander* Pope.

BILLIE. "The proper study of —— "

PAUL. " —— mankind is man."

BILLIE. "—mankind is man." Of course, that means womenkind, too?

PAUL. Yes.

BILLIE. (*Impatiently.*) Yes, I know.

PAUL. Don't worry about books so much. (SHE *blows her nose. The tears end.*)

BILLIE. I *been* studying different mankind lately. The ones you told me? Jane Addams last week, and this week Tom Paine. And then all by myself I got to thinkin' about Harry. Like he works so hard to get what he wants. For instance. But he doesn't know what he wants.

PAUL. More of what he's got, probably.

BILLIE. Money.

PAUL. Money, more people to push around, money.

BILLIE. Well, he's not so bad as you think he is.

PAUL. I know. He's got a brain of gold. (*Sound of key in door.* BROCK *comes in.*)

BROCK. Hello.

PAUL. Hello, Harry. We were just talking about you.

BROCK. (*Removing hat and coat and putting them on chair L. of door.*) Yeah? Well, that ain't what I pay ya for. (*Goes to chair R. of door, looks through mail, selects large envelope.*) She knows enough about me. Too much, in fact. (*Crossing to chair L. of desk.*) Ed here?

BILLIE. No.

BROCK. God damn it! He's supposed to meet me. (PAUL *and* BILLIE *watch as* HE *sits and takes off his shoes.*)

PAUL. (*To* BILLIE.) What did you find out about Tom Paine?

BILLIE. Well, he was quite a fella.

PAUL. Where was he born, do you remember?

BILLIE. London? No. Or England. Some place like that.

BROCK. What d'you mean London *or* England? It's the same thing.

BILLIE. It is?

BROCK. London is *in* England. It's a city, London. England's a whole country.

BILLIE. I forgot.

BROCK. (*To* PAUL.) Honest to God, boy! You got some patience!

PAUL. Take it easy.

BROCK. How can anybody get so dumb?

PAUL. We can't all know everything, Harry.

BILLIE. (*To* BROCK.) Who's Tom Paine, for instance?

BROCK. What?

BILLIE. You heard me. Tom Paine?

BROCK. What the hell do I care who he is?

BILLIE. *I* know.

BROCK. So what? If I wanted to know who he is so I'd know who he is. I just don't care. (*To* PAUL.) Go ahead. Don't let me butt in.

PAUL. (*To* BILLIE.) Which of his books did you like best?

BILLIE. Well, I didn't read *by* him, yet—only *about* him.

PAUL. Oh.

BILLIE. But I made a list of —— (*She turns to get pad from end table.*)

BROCK. (*Interrupting suddenly.*) Who's Rabbit Maranville?

BILLIE. (*Turning quickly.*) Who?

BROCK. (*Over-enunciating.*) Rabbit Maranville.
BILLIE. I don' know any *rabbits!*
BROCK. . . . think you're so smart.
PAUL. Used to play shortstop for the Braves, didn't he?
BROCK. (*To* PAUL.) What're you? Some kind of a genius?
PAUL. No.
BROCK. (*Rising, crossing behind desk.*) I hire and fire geniuses
every day.
PAUL. I'm sure you do. (HE *turns to* BILLIE.) Where's that....?
BILLIE. (*Handing over her list.*) Here. (BROCK *crosses* D.R. *to
front of desk, thinking hard.*)
PAUL. (*Studying list.*) Well, suppose you start with "The Age of
Reason."
BILLIE. (*Writing it down.*) "The-Age-of-Reason."
PAUL. Then, next, you might ——
BROCK. (*Front of desk.*) Who's Willie Hop?
PAUL. (*Turning slightly.*) National billiard champion. And it's
pronounced —— Hoppé.
BROCK. That's what I said. Anyways, I didn't ask *you.* I asked *her.*
(*He crosses* R. *and behind desk.*)
PAUL. Sorry. (*He turns back to* BILLIE.) Where were we?
BILLIE (*With a look of disgust in* BROCK's *direction.*) "Age of
Reason."
PAUL. All right, then try "The Rights of Man."
BILLIE. (*Writing.*) "The-Rights-of-Man." (BROCK *slowly
crosses to* C.)
PAUL. I think that'll give you a rough idea of what ——
BROCK. (*Suddenly, crossing to them.*) What's a peninsula?
BILLIE (*Waving him off.*) Sshhh!!
BROCK. Don't give me that Sshhh ——! You think you know so
much —— *what's* a *peninsula?*
PAUL. It's a ——
BROCK. Not you.
BILLIE. (*Confidently and with condescending superiority.*) It's that
new medicine!!! (BROCK *turns away, throwing up his hands in
surrender, crosses to front of desk,* D.R. *then comes back to sofa.*)
BROCK. It is not!
BILLIE. What then?
BROCK. (*As a schoolboy, arms stiffly at his sides.*) It's a body of
land surrounded on three sides by water. (*He relaxes.*)
BILLIE. So what's *that* to know?

BROCK. So what's this —— this Sam Paine to know?
BILLIE. (*Straightening up.*) Some difference! *Tom* Paine —— not *Sam* Paine — *Tom* Paine practically started this whole country.
BROCK. You mean he's dead?
BILLIE. Of course.
BROCK. (*Yelling at* PAUL.) What the hell you learnin' her about *dead* people? I just want her to know how to act with *live* people!
PAUL. Education's pretty hard to control, Harry. One thing leads to another. It's a matter of awakening curiosity—imagination— independence—first thing you know—
BROCK. (*Crossing* R. *to chair* L. *of desk.*) Work on *her*, not me.
PAUL. No extra charge.
BROCK. I don't need nothin' you can tell me.
PAUL. (*With meaning.*) Oh, I'm sure we could tell each other lots of interesting things, Harry.
BROCK. What the hell's *that* mean?
PAUL. Just trying to be friendly.
BROCK. (*Crossing to chair* L. *of desk and sitting.*) Who asked ya? You know, the more I see you I don't like you as much. For a chump who's got no place, you're pretty fresh. You better watch out—I got an eye on you.
PAUL. All right. Let's both watch out.
BROCK. If I wanted I could knock your block off if I wanted.
PAUL. Yes, I know.
BROCK. All right, then—just go ahead and do what you're sup- posed—and that's all.
PAUL. Well, we'll stop for now.
BROCK. (*With honest interest.*) No, go ahead. I wanna see how you do it. (*Settles back and waits.*)
PAUL. (*Rising and moving to door.*) Not just now if you don't mind—I've got to go lie down. (*He stops, turns back.*) You don't realize how hard I work.
BILLIE. Ha ha! Some joke.
BROCK. (*Victimized.*) Two hundred bucks a week and I can't even watch! (*Rises and crosses back of desk.*)
PAUL. . . . take you on separately, Harry. Glad to. I've got a special course for backward millionaires! (HE *goes.* BROCK *cannot decide whether or not he has been insulted.* HE *puts his attention on the material in large envelope.* BILLIE *curls up with her "David Cop- perfield."*)
BROCK. (*Looking at* BILLIE *pityingly.*) London *or* England! Hon-

61

est to God! (BILLIE *snoots him. He returns to work, which consists of examining fat legal documents.*)

BILLIE. (*Looking up.*) Harry ——

BROCK. (*Absorbed.*) Yeah?

BILLIE. What's this business we're in down here? Could you tell me?

BROCK. What d'you mean *we?*

BILLIE. Well, I figure I'm a sort of a partner, in a way.

BROCK. A silent partner.

BILLIE. So?

BROCK. (*Looking at her.*) So *shut up!*

BILLIE. I got a right to know.

BROCK. You got a right to get the hell outa my hair. Just put your nose in your book and keep it. (*Sits on desk back to her.*)

BILLIE. (*Turning her back to him.*) I don' wanna do anything if it's against the law. That's one sure thing. (*Back to book.*)

BROCK. You'll do what I tell ya.

BILLIE. I think I know what it is, only I'm not sure.

BROCK. You should worry. You're doin' all right. Sump'n you want you ain't got maybe?

BILLIE. Yuh.

BROCK. (*Not looking at her.*) What?

BILLIE. (*Musing.*) I wanna be like the happy peasant.

BROCK. (*Turning and yelling.*) I'll *buy* it for you! (HELEN *enters from service wing, carrying book. Crosses* L. *to bookcase.*) Now will you stop crabbin'? (HELEN *puts book on bookshelf.*)

HELEN. Well, I finished finally. Thanks loads for the loan of it.

BILLIE. (*Giving* HELEN *her full attention.*) How'd you like it?

HELEN. (*Coming down to* R. *of sofa for a chat.*) Pretty punk.

BILLIE. Really, Helen? I enjoyed it.

HELEN. Not me. I don't go for these stories where it shows how miserable it is to be rich.

BILLIE. Well, it *can* be if a person ——

BROCK. (*Standing, annoyed.*) All right! Can the coffee-klotch. (*To* HELEN.) Knock off!

HELEN. Sorry, Mr. Brock. (*She leaves, quickly, with a little see-you-later wave to* BILLIE.)

BROCK. Don't get so pally with everybody.

BILLIE. (*Starting a crescendo.*) Paul says it's all right.

BROCK. Never mind *Paul* says. *I* don't like it.

BILLIE. (*Rising to her knees, in heat.*) You know what you are?

BROCK. (*Crossing to her.*) What? (THEY *face each other challengingly.*)

BILLIE. Uh—(*Unable to think of the suitable barb, she jumps to large dictionary and starts looking up word, furiously. Door buzzer.* EDDIE *comes in and crosses to main door.* BILLIE *finds what she has been looking for. She looks up from dictionary.*) Antisocial!

BROCK. You're goddamn right I am! (*Goes back to desk.* EDDIE *opens door to admit* DEVERY *and* HEDGES. *Picks up* BROCK'S *coat and hat from chair* L. *of main door.*)

DEVERY. (*Coming in.*) Good evening.

BROCK. Where the hell you guys been? You know what time it is?

DEVERY. Sorry.

BROCK. You're always sorry.

HEDGES. (*Coming in.*) My fault. (*To* BILLIE.) Good evening.

BILLIE. Good evening. (*Motioning, and speaking as though coached.*) Won't you sit down?

HEDGES. (*Sitting.*) Thank you.

DEVERY. (C.) How are you, Billie?

BILLIE. Superb. New word! (*She sits, happily.* EDDIE *crosses to chair* L. *of desk, picks up* BROCK'S *shoes, takes them upstairs.*)

BROCK. (*Impatiently.*) All right all right! What happened? (*An awkward pause.* DEVERY *and* HEDGES *exchange a look and silently gird their loins.*)

HEDGES. (*Softly.*) It's just this, Harry . . . may take a little more time and—(HE *pauses.*)

DEVERY. (*Picking it up.*)—and a little more money.

BROCK. (*Angrily.*) Why?

DEVERY. Well, for one thing, the whole amendment has to be re-drafted.

BROCK. (*Moving to* DEVERY.) I don't want no re-drafted and I don't wanna wait.

HEDGES. I'm afraid you'll have to.

BROCK. (*Crossing to between* DEVERY *and* HEDGES.) Don't tell *me* what I *have* to!

HEDGES. If you'd let me ——

BROCK. (*His finger in* HEDGES' *face.*) Listen, I don't like you. You're makin' me feel like some sucker.

DEVERY. (*Placating.*) I'm sure Norval's doing his best.

BROCK. (*Looking at* HEDGES.) Well, his best ain't good enough.

63

DEVERY. Don't be unreasonable, Harry. (BROCK *turns to* HIM.) There're ninety-six votes up there. Norval's just one guy. (EDDIE *comes down and goes out to service wing.*)

BROCK. Well, he's the *wrong* guy. What the hell—we've handled it before!

HEDGES. (*Weakly.*) Things aren't the same.

BROCK. (*To* DEVERY.) We'll make 'em the same. (*To* HEDGES.) That's your job, ain't it?

DEVERY. Pretty tough assignment.

BROCK. (*To* DEVERY.) What do I care? (*To* HEDGES.) And you! You better get movin' or I'll butcher you! You'll wind up a goddamn Y.M.C.A. secretary again before you know it.

DEVERY. (*Shocked.*) Harry!

BROCK. I'm gonna get it fixed so's I can do business *where* I want and *how* I want and as *big* as I want. If you ain't *with* me, you're *against* me.

HEDGES. I'm with you.

BROCK. All *right* then! (*Turning and stalking upstairs.*) You'll have to pull your weight in the goddamn boat or I'll get somebody who can. You hear me good? (HE *goes into his room and slams door. Awkward pause.*)

HEDGES. (*Softly.*) . . . quite a temper, hasn't he?

DEVERY. Don't mind him, he's always lived at the top of his voice. (*Crossing* L. *to liquor. Pours drink.*) Anybody with me? Norval?

HEDGES. No, thank you.

BILLIE. (*To* HEDGES, *softly.*) I don't think Harry should talk to you like that. After all, you're a Senator.

HEDGES. (*A worried sigh.*) Oh well—

BILLIE. I don't think *anybody* should talk to a Senator like that —— or be *able* to! A Senator's a wonderful thing.

HEDGES. Thank you.

BILLIE. (*With a serious little frown.*) The way it looks to me —— if he pushes *you* around, it's like he's pushing a few million people around.

HEDGES. How do you mean?

BILLIE. The people who picked you.

HEDGES. Well, not quite that many.

BILLIE. How many then?

HEDGES. Eight hundred six thousand, four hundred and thirty-four.

BILLIE. Well, *that's* quite a few to push around.

64

HEDGES. *You're* not one of my constituents by any chance, are you?

BILLIE. (*Thinks a moment, then looks at dictionary stand, wishfully.*) I don't think I know that one yet?

DEVERY. The Senator means are you one of the people who voted for him?

BILLIE. Oh. I never voted for anybody.

HEDGES. Why not?

BILLIE. I don't know. I wouldn't know how to, I guess.

DEVERY. (*Coming down to back of sofa, between them.*) Simple. You just press a button.

BILLIE. Yuh, but which one? Like suppose it's between different people?

DEVERY. (*Smiling.*) Well, you listen to the speeches —— you read the papers —— you make up your own mind. You take a look and see who's for who —— that's *very* important. Once you take a stand on something —— take a look and see who's on the other side and who's on *your* side. (DEVERY *crosses* R. *to* C.—*stands watching* BILLIE *and* HEDGES.)

HEDGES. (*Lightly.*) That's all there is to it.

BILLIE. (*To* HEDGES.) Yuh, but why do you take it from Harry? That's what I wanna know. You're more important than him. You're a Senator!

HEDGES. Yes, and as such, you see, I have a great many duties and responsibilities and —— (*He stops.*)

BILLIE. Yuh?

HEDGES. (*Stalling.*) The operation of government is—uh—very complex.

BILLIE. Why should it be? I understand it pretty good in the books and when Paul tells me —— but then when I see a thing like this ——it's like different.

HEDGES. How?

BILLIE. Well, when it comes down to what should be laws and what shouldn't —— is Harry more important than anybody else?

HEDGES. (*Meaning yes.*) No.

BILLIE. Then how come he's got so much to say? Who ever voted for *him*?

HEDGES. (*Rising.*) Well, we'll have a nice long talk about it some time.

BILLIE. (*Seriously.*) All right.

HEDGES. Good-bye.

BILLIE. Good-bye. (HEDGES *goes to door.* DEVERY *follows.* BILLIE *goes to large dictionary and looks up "constituent".* HEDGES *regards her as* DEVERY *hands him his hat.*)

HEDGES. Quite a little girl.

DEVERY. Oh, yes!

HEDGES. Good-bye.

DEVERY. See you. (HEDGES *goes.* DEVERY *picks up brief-case, takes out sheaf of papers. Comes down* C.) Few things here for you. (*Crosses to desk, spreads papers out for signing.* BILLIE *comes over. She picks up her glasses. He hands her his fountain pen, then goes and pours another drink.* BILLIE *stands looking at paper. Puts on her glasses and starts to read top one, carefully. A moment later,* DEVERY *turns back into room. He stops and looks at* BILLIE *in surprise. Then crosses* C.)

BILLIE. (*Quietly.*) What is this?

DEVERY. Same old stuff.

BILLIE. What?

DEVERY. (*Putting her off.*) Take too long to explain.

BILLIE. No, it wouldn't. I like having things explained to me. I found that out.

DEVERY. Some other time.

BILLIE. Now.

DEVERY. (*Crossing to her.*) You want me to tell Harry?

BILLIE. Tell him what?

DEVERY. That you won't sign this stuff?

BILLIE. Who said anything about that? I just wanna know what it is.

DEVERY. A merger.

BILLIE. What's that?

DEVERY. Several companies being formed into one.

BILLIE. All Harry's?

DEVERY. No.

BILLIE. Whose, then?

DEVERY. A few of Harry's and some others. French, Italian and so on.

BILLIE. (*Whipping off glasses, suddenly.*) A *cartel!!* (DEVERY *looks at her, amazed.*)

DEVERY. What are you talking about?

BILLIE. About cartels. If that's what this is then I'm against it. Paul explained me the whole thing. (*She drops papers as though afraid of contamination.* DEVERY *is dumbfounded. He stalls.*)

DEVERY. It's perfectly all right. Don't worry.

BILLIE. You sure?

DEVERY. Ask Harry.

BILLIE. All right.

DEVERY. He won't like it.

BILLIE. Why not?

DEVERY. He just won't, that's all. He doesn't like people butting in.

BILLIE. I'm not people.

DEVERY. Listen to me, Billie. Be smart.

BILLIE. How can I be smart if nobody ever tells me anything?

DEVERY. *I'm* telling you something.

BILLIE. What?

DEVERY. Sign the stuff and don't start up with him.

BILLIE. (*Putting pen down.*) Tomorrow.

DEVERY. Why tomorrow?

BILLIE. I wanna look 'em over, so I'll know what I'm doing.

DEVERY. (*Losing his temper.*) It's all right!

BILLIE. Must be something fishy. If not, you'd tell me.

DEVERY. Take my word for it.

BILLIE. No. (DEVERY *is uncomfortable and shows it. Tries hard to think of another approach.*) I know what you feel bad about. You don't like to be doin' all his dirty work —— because you know you're better than him.

DEVERY. (*White.*) That's enough.

BILLIE. (*Plunging ahead, loudly.*) But I'm not so sure — maybe you're worse! (DEVERY *looks at her for a moment, then goes upstairs and into* BROCK'S *room, in angry determination.* BILLIE *looks up at* BROCK'S *door, picks up papers and dictionary and brings them to sofa. Picks up papers and reads. A word baffles her. She looks it up. Then picks up papers again. Now* BROCK *appears on balcony, coatless, sleeves rolled up. He is smoking a cigarette and wears slippers. Comes down into room, slowly.* BILLIE *does not look up, but continues what she is doing.* BROCK *crosses room. She senses his silent fury as he passes behind her. Crosses to liquor and gets drink. Then crosses to chair* L. *of desk and sits down, facing* BILLIE. *She is frightened.* BROCK *gives no sign of anger or violence. He watches her. Finally he breaks the silence.*)

BROCK. (*Quietly.*) Innarresting?

BILLIE. (*Without looking up.*) Not very.

BROCK. I suppose you're used to readin' more high-tone stuff?

BILLIE. Yes, I am. (*Another long pause.*)

BROCK. (*Gently.*) What's a matter, kid?

BILLIE. Nothing.

BROCK. All of a sudden?

BILLIE. (*Looks at* BROCK.) I don't like that Ed.

BROCK. Why, what'd he do to you?

BILLIE. He didn't do nothin'—*anything* to me. It's what he's done to himself.

BROCK. Done what?

BILLIE. He used to be the Assistant Attorney General of the whole United States.

BROCK. Who?

BILLIE. Ed.

BROCK. So what's wrong with that?

BILLIE. Nothing's wrong. Just look at him now. (BROCK *is puzzled.*) You know he once wrote a book? "The Roots of Freedom." That was the name of it. I read it. It was beautyful.

BROCK. Where'd you get all this?

BILLIE. I looked it up.

BROCK. Why?

BILLIE. No reason. I was just in the library. And look at him now. He hangs around and helps you promote, and lets you walk all over him just because you pay 'im for it.

BROCK. Oh, so we finally got around to me!

BILLIE. Yuh. I'm not sure I like *you*, either. You're selfish, that's your trouble.

BROCK. Since when is all this?

BILLIE. Since now.

BROCK. You don't say!

BILLIE. I used to think you were a big man, Harry. No more. All through history there's been bigger men than you, and better. Now, too.

BROCK. Who, for instance?

BILLIE. Thousands.

BROCK. Name one.

BILLIE. (*After a moment.*) My father.

BROCK. (*Contemptuously.*) Twenty-five a week.

BILLIE. (*Looking at him.*) "—brain of gold."

BROCK. (*Confused.*) What?

BILLIE. Never mind.

BROCK. (*Rising, moving to her and advising kindly.*) Listen, cutie, don't get nervous just because you read a book. (*Reassuring her.*) *You're* as dumb as you ever were. (*Sits near her.*)

BILLIE. You think so?
BROCK. Sure, but I don't mind. You know why? (HE *inches closer.*)
Because you've got the best little —— (HE *lunges at her rudely.*)
BILLIE. (*Springing away and crossing* R. *back of desk, with a shud-
der.*) Leave me *alone*, Harry! (*The tempo of their exchange ac-
celerates.*)
BROCK. Come *here!*
BILLIE. No!!
BROCK. (*Loud.*) I never seen you like this.
BILLIE. (*Pacing, matching his tone.*) I never *been* like this. I feel
like I wanna go 'way some place.
BROCK. Where?
BILLIE. I don't *know!*
BROCK. I may wind up here in a few weeks. We'll go to Florida
maybe.
BILLIE. I mean *alone!*
BROCK. You know what I think? I think you've gone nuts!
BILLIE. Maybe!
BROCK. Calm down!
BILLIE. I can't!
BROCK. Why not?
BILLIE. (D.R. *of desk, passionately.*) I don't know. I just know I
hate my life. There's a better kind I know it. If you read some of
these books *you'd* know it, too. Maybe it's right what you say I'm
still dumb. But I know one thing I never knew before. There's a
better kind of life than the one I got. Or you.
BROCK. (*Rising and going to her.*) I suppose you figure you'da
been better off with that lousy saxophone player?
BILLIE. At least he was honest! (*Toe to toe, front of desk.*)
BROCK. He was a dime-a-dozen chump.
BILLIE. He worked for a livin', that's one thing ——
BROCK. (*Outraged.*) *I* work. I been workin' since I was twelve
years old —— nobody ever give me nothin'.
BILLIE. If a man goes and robs a house —— *that's* work, too.
BROCK. In my whole life—— (HELEN, *carrying towels, enters
from service wing.* BROCK *stops, abruptly.* HELEN, *sensing
charged a,mosphere, quickens her pace as she goes upstairs.* BILLIE
and BROCK *watch her go. The moment she disappears they swing
back to each other and continue the fray.*) In my whole life I
never robbed a house! What the hell you talkin' about?
BILLIE. (*Patronizingly.*) You can hardly understand anything, can

69

you?

BROCK. Get off that high horse—— you dumb little pot!

BILLIE. (*Closer to him.*) You —— (*Tries hard to think of something worse.*) —— menace!

BROCK. (*Crossing* D.L. *to sofa.*) I picked you up out of the gutter and I can throw you back there, too. (*Turning to her.*) Why, you never had a decent *meal* before you met me.

BILLIE. (*Crossing* L. *to* BROCK, *face to face with him.*) Yeah, but I had to have 'em with *you.* You eat terrible! You got no manners. Takin' your shoes off all the time —— that's another thing . . . and pickin' your teeth. . . . (*Turning away haughtily.*) You're *just* —— not —— *couth!* (HELEN *comes down stairs, goes out service entrance.* BROCK *waits until she has gone.*)

BROCK. (*Shouting.*) I'm couther than you are!

BILLIE. (*Crossing* R. *to below of desk.*) And that cheap per*fume* you put on yourself.

BROCK. Cheap?! I don't own *nothin'* cheap. Except *you!*

BILLIE. (*Deeply hurt, she turns to him and speaks with quiet strength.*) You don't own me. Nobody can own anybody. There's a law says.

BROCK. (*Loudly.*) Don't tell me about the law! If I was scared of the law, I wouldn't be where I am.

BILLIE. Where are you?

BROCK. All right, you've talked enough. If you don't like it here, beat it. You'll be back. (BILLIE *starts upstairs.*) Wait a minute. (HE *gets papers from coffee table, crosses* R. *to desk.*) First this.

BILLIE. (*At foot of stairs.*) Not now.

BROCK. *(Turning to her.) Right now.*

BILLIE. No!

BROCK. (*Loud.*) C'mere!

BILLIE. (*Determined.*) I'm not gonna sign anything any more till I know what I'm signing. From now on.

BROCK. (*Out of control.*) Do what I'm tellin' ya! (HE *pounds desk.* BILLIE *stands rigid and scared, but manages a small, grim shake of her head.* BROCK *moves slowly to her.* HE *is suddenly in front of her. Raises his arm.*)

BILLIE. (*Cringing.*) Harry, please! Don't (HER *last word is cut in two by a stinging slap! which buckles her knees. A cry escapes her as he strikes her again. The seed of her rebellion is suddently uprooted. She sags and sobs, defeated.* BROCK *propels her to desk in a series of rough shoves. Still sobbing, she follows his di-*

rection and signs documents, one by one. When she has finished,
BILLIE'*s head goes to her folded arms on desk.* BROCK *takes papers,*
crosses L. *to sofa, puts them down, turns to her.*)
BROCK. (*Back of sofa.*) All right, now get the hell outa here.
BILLIE. What?
BROCK. (*Bellowing.*) Don't be bawlin' around here, that's what. I
don't like it. I been treatin' you too good, that's the trouble. You
don't appreciate it. Nothin'. I ain't gonna have nobody around
here who don't know their place. So get the hell outa here. Go sit
on a park bench some place till you're ready to behave yourself.
(BILLIE *doesn't move.*) Go on!! (BILLIE *rises brokenly, starts for*
stairs. BROCK *points to front door.*) This way out!
BILLIE. (*At foot of stairs, in small voice.*) I gotta put somethin' on.
BROCK. Well, hurry up! I don't want you around here like this.
(*Turning to pour drink.*) Ya *bother* me! (HE *drinks.* BILLIE *starts*
up. Halfway there, she stops, turns.)
BILLIE. (*Loud and bitter.*) Big— Fascist!
BROCK. (*Turning to her.*) What? (SHE *runs up quickly, goes into*
her room. BROCK *takes another drink. His attention goes to stack of*
books before him. Instantly he identifies it as the root of his prob-
lem. He pushes them to the floor, violently, finding a strange re-
lease in this. Kicks them out of his way and crosses to desk.
Picks up one of the books on corner of desk and throws it to floor,
U.C. *Then another. Picks up another, tears it in half. There is*
mingled fury, excitement and satisfaction in his heart as he com-
pletes destruction of book. Starts on another, as DEVERY *appears on*
balcony. BROCK *stops, as though discovered in an indecent act,*
lets book drop to floor.)
DEVERY. (*On steps.*) All set?
BROCK. (*Crossing to sofa, getting papers, handing them to* ED.)
Certainly all set. What'd you think—I'm gonna let a broad talk
back? (*He sits.*)
DEVERY. Where is she?
BROCK. I told her take a walk. One thing I can't stand it's a crier.
DEVERY. (*Crossing to him.*) What's she crying about?
BROCK. What do I know?
DEVERY. (*With a sigh.*) . . . becoming a strange girl.
BROCK. She's all right. All this book stuff's got her nervous, that's
all.
DEVERY. (*Crossing to chair* L. *of desk. Softly.*) "A little learning
is a dangerous thing."

71

BROCK. What!?

DEVERY. Nothing, Harry. (*Sitting.*) Looks as though your passion for educating her was a mistake.

BROCK. I didn't know it woulda turned out like *this*, did I? . . . Remind me to fire that four-eyed Verrall skunk.

DEVERY. Why blame him?

BROCK. He must of told her *too* much. (*A pause.*) You know what she called me before? A *fatch*-ist.

DEVERY. (*Almost smiling.*) She did?

BROCK. It don't make sense. I was born in Plainfield, New Jersey. *She* knows that. (*Shakes his head dejectedly.*)

DEVERY. What's the matter, Harry?

BROCK. (*Softer.*) I love that broad. (*A pause.* BROCK *appears to be thinking hard. Looks up, suddenly.*) Hey! You think we could maybe find somebody to make her *dumb* again? (BILLIE *comes down, dressed for the street, and moves toward front door. As she opens it* BROCK *bellows without turning.*) And don't be late if you don't want a bloody nose! (BILLIE *stops, turns, moves a step into room.*)

BILLIE. (*Ever so gently.*) Would you do me a favor, Harry?

BROCK. (*Mean, still not looking at her.*) What?

BILLIE. Drop dead? (SHE *leaves quickly, closes door behind her, before* BROCK *comes to. He does so with a snap! Looks at* DEVERY, *then rises slowly and is turning to door, flabbergasted.*)

CURTAIN

ACT III

SCENE: *The same. Later that evening,* DEVERY, *coatless, sits on sofa, working on a pile of documents.* HE *is somewhat drunker than before.* BROCK, *in pajamas and dressing-gown, is pacing the floor.*

BROCK. What time is it a'ready?

DEVERY. (*Looking at his watch.*) One-thirty.

BROCK. (*Crossing* R. *to behind desk.*) I'll slug 'er senseless when she comes back.

DEVERY. *If.*

BROCK. Listen, I had this before with 'er. She always winds up where I want 'er.

DEVERY. I hope so. (*A pause.*)

BROCK. What time is it?

DEVERY. One-thirty.

BROCK. (*Crossing to* D.L. *corner of desk.*) You said that before.

DEVERY. One thirty-one.

BROCK. What time she go out?

DEVERY. I don't know. Five, six o'clock.

BROCK. (*Crossing to* C.) Eight hours.

DEVERY. What?

BROCK. She's been gone eight hours.

DEVERY. Maybe she's seeing a double-feature.

BROCK. (*Crossing* R. *to desk.*) Yeah. (*A pause.*) *That* don't take eight hours! (*Crossing to sofa.*) She coulda got into an accident.

DEVERY. You'd hear.

BROCK. She coulda got *raped!* (DEVERY *looks at him, quizzically.*) It happens all the time.

DEVERY. Not to Billie. Maybe the other way around, but not to Billie.

BROCK. (*Pacing again.*) You'd think Eddie'd call up at least. . . .

DEVERY. Be damned inconvenient if he doesn't find her. I've got some more to be signed. It can't wait. (EDDIE *comes in.*)

EDDIE. She here?

BROCK. What d'you mean she here? *No!*

EDDIE. The guy downstairs said he seen 'er go out then he seen 'er come in.

BROCK. He's blind. Go look some more.

EDDIE. (*Coming into room, protesting.*) I been all over town.

BROCK. Well, go over it *again!* (*The slightest possible hesitation from* EDDIE.) Do what I'm tellin' ya!!

EDDIE. (*Bouncing.*) Sure. (*Going out to service wing.*) Just change my socks.

DEVERY. (*Looking upstairs.*) If I thought I could make those stairs I'd go lie down.

BROCK. (*Sitting chair* L. *of desk.*) I sure never thought she was gonna turn out like this.

DEVERY. . . . you thought any more about that matter we discussed in connection with her?

BROCK. What connection?

73

DEVERY. Marrying her?

BROCK. Still harpin', huh?

DEVERY. (*Rising, crossing to* BROCK.) . . . gone beyond the reasons of appearance, Harry—if she's going to be truculent, I'm thinking of your legal safety. On paper she owns —

BROCK. (*Hard.*) I *know* what she owns!

DEVERY. (*Leaning over him.*) You've *got* to *do* it, Harry. (*Long pause.* BROCK *crosses to liquor.*)

BROCK. They always hook ya in the end, them broads. (*Pours drink.*) It's crazy, y'know it?

DEVERY. (U.L. *of desk.*) How?

BROCK. (*Back of sofa.*) A whole trouble account of a dame reads a book.

DEVERY. Just goes to show you.

BROCK. Yeah. (HE *drinks.*)

DEVERY. (*Crossing to* BROCK.) It's the new world, Harry . . . Force and reason changing places. Knowledge is power. You can lead a horse to water.

BROCK. What?

DEVERY. Honesty is the best policy. A stitch in time saves nine. (*Starts upstairs. Trips on bottom step. Recovers, leans on balustrade.*)

BROCK. (*Moving to him.*) I don' like the way things are goin' around here. *You* stewed all the time—the broad outa line— and that's some fine Senator y'bought me!

DEVERY. I think he's cute.

BROCK. I could get me a better Senator outa The Automat.

DEVERY. Best I could do.

BROCK. I'd like to trade 'im in, no kíddin'.

DEVERY. They're not all for sale, Harry. That's the trouble with this town—too many honest men in it. (DEVERY *goes upstairs and into* BROCK'S *room.* BROCK *paces, lights cigarette—then stops, stares at books. Crosses to desk. Picks up two books, weighs them, selects the lighter and moves to sofa. Reads, with some difficulty, his lips forming the words.* EDDIE *comes in.*)

EDDIE. I'll take a look downstairs and see if she's———(HE *stops abruptly at sight of* BROCK, *who turns to see him gaping.*)

BROCK. (*Challengingly.*) What's a matter?

EDDIE. Nuthin'.

BROCK. Didn't you ever see a person readin' a book, for Christ sake?

EDDIE. Sure.

BROCK. All right then. Get the hell outa here!

EDDIE. Sure. (HE *goes quietly.* BROCK *reads. He has difficulty holding the continuity as he turns a page. Turns it back and forth several times, last time speedily, in an attempt to capture the thread. Behind him door opens noiselessly and* BILLIE *looks in.* SHE *closes door.* BROCK *reads a bit longer, then gives up. Tears book in two and throws it away. Rises, goes upstairs. Turns out main light from balcony and goes into his room.* BILLIE *comes in, looks around. Goes upstairs, stops at* BROCK'S *door, listens. Then comes down to main door.* SHE *motions* PAUL *to come in.* HE *closes door.* BILLIE *moves to desk.* SHE *searches.* PAUL *waits* U.C., *watching* BROCK'S *door.* BILLIE *holds letter out to* PAUL. HE *takes it, examines it carefully, nods. Quietly, systematically, they go through desk.* PAUL *collects a pile of documents, letters, checkbooks, and material he wants.* BILLIE *crosses and picks up what was left by* DEVERY *on coffee table.* PAUL *follows her.* SHE *hands it over,* HE *examines it, nods.*)

BILLIE. (*Whispering.*) Okay?

PAUL. (*Quietly.*) . . . ought to do it fine.

BILLIE. I probably won't see you again, Paul ——

PAUL. (*Full voice.*) What!?

BILLIE. Sssh!

PAUL. (*A whisper.*) What?!

BILLIE. So I want to say goodbye and thanks for everything.

PAUL. Where are you going?

BILLIE. Just away from here, that's all I know.

PAUL. Where? You can tell *me.*

BILLIE. I don't know. I thought I might go see my father for a while.

PAUL. And have a hot lunch every day?

BILLIE. Yeah.

PAUL. I've got a better idea.

BILLIE. What?

PAUL. Let's get married.

BILLIE. You must be daffy.

PAUL. I love you, Billie.

BILLIE. You don't love *me.* You just love my *brain.*

PAUL. That, too.

BILLIE. What would the boss of The New Republic say?

PAUL. I don't know. Probably congratulations.

75

BILLIE. I'll think it over, but I can tell you now the answer's no. (PAUL *kisses her.*) What're you doing?

PAUL. Well, if you don't know, I must be doing it wrong. (*Kisses her again.*)

BILLIE. (*Sitting.*) What's more important right now—crabbin' Harry's act or romancing?

PAUL. (*Sitting beside her.*) Both.

BILLIE. Honest, Paul—I wish you'd—(*Door opens suddenly and* EDDIE *comes in.* HE *snaps switch, flooding room with light.* PAUL *and* BILLIE *rise.* PAUL *crosses to front of desk, removing lipstick from his face with handkerchief.*)

EDDIE. What's this? Night school? (*To* BILLIE.) Where were you, anyway? I looked all over town.

BILLIE. I walked over to the White House and back.

EDDIE. How's everybody over there? (*To* PAUL.) Better knock off, Buster.

PAUL. Why?

EDDIE. (*Indicating* BROCK'S *room.*) I'm supposed to tell 'im she's back. I don't think he'll like it you horsin' around with his girl in the middle of the night. He's funny that way.

PAUL. I'll take a chance.

BILLIE. You better go.

EDDIE. Take advice.

PAUL. What's it to *you?*

EDDIE. (*Starting upstairs.*) Listen, noise I can stand but blood makes me nervous. (*Goes into* BROCK'S *room.*)

BILLIE. (*Crossing to* PAUL.) Please, Paul.

PAUL. . . . sure you'll be all right?

BILLIE. Don't worry.

PAUL. Goodbye, Billie.

BILLIE. Goodbye. (PAUL *kisses her quickly and goes.* BILLIE *stands alone for a moment, then moves to desk, picks up phone.*) Porter, please. (SHE *sorts out a few things on desk.*) Hello, porter . . . This is 67D. Could you send up somebody for my bags? . . . No, right now . . . Thank you. (EDDIE *comes out of* BROCK'S *room, rubbing his stomach.*)

EDDIE. (*Gasping.*) Ooh! (*Stands on balcony, bent over.*)

BILLIE. What's the matter?

EDDIE. Right in the stomach he hit me.

BILLIE. Why didn't you hit him back?

EDDIE. What?

BILLIE. Why didn't you hit him back?

EDDIE. (*Leaning over balcony rail.*) He's been sayin' you've gone nuts. I could believe it, you know it?

BILLIE. Do me a favor?

EDDIE. What?

BILLIE. Pack me up up there?

EDDIE. You scrammin' again?

BILLIE. For good.

EDDIE. I tell you the truth, I'm sorry. I think *he's* gonna be sorry, too.

BILLIE. He's gonna be worse than sorry.

EDDIE. Where you goin'?

BILLIE. Never mind.

EDDIE. You sore at *me*, too?

BILLIE. In a way.

EDDIE. What'd *I* do? What'd I *do?*

BILLIE. It's a new thing with me. I'm gonna be sore at anybody who *takes* it. From now on.

EDDIE. (*With a frown.*) Listen, don' get me thinkin', I got enough trouble now. (HE *goes into* BILLIE'S *room.* SHE *begins to sort out her belongings at desk.* BROCK *appears.*)

BROCK. (*Coming downstairs.*) Fine time!

BILLIE. (*Gay.*) Hello, Harry.

BROCK. Where you been?

BILLIE. I took a walk like you told me.

BROCK. That took you till now?

BILLIE. What's a matter, Harry? You miss me?

BROCK. (*Close to her.*) I decided sump'n to tell you. Sump'n good. I don' like to wait when I get an idea.

BILLIE. Yuh, I know.

BROCK. (*Crossing* L. *to front of sofa.*) Now I see you, I don' know if I should tell you it.

BILLIE. Why not?

BROCK. Runnin' out, talkin' fresh, slammin' doors. I knew you'd be back, though.

BILLIE. You did, huh?

BROCK. I told Ed, even. He got worried. Not me.

BILLIE. Not yet.

BROCK. What took you so long?

BILLIE. I had a lot to think.

BROCK. For instance?

BILLIE. Just where I stand around here.

BROCK. (*A step to her.*) That's what I'm tryin' to tell ya.

BILLIE. What?

BROCK. Where you stand.

BILLIE. Yuh.

BROCK. (*Crossing to her.*) Well—first thing, that Verrall stuff is out. It gets in my way—and I don' like you upset so much. It's bad for you. And the next thing—we're gonna get married.

BILLIE. No.

BROCK. Only you gotta behave yourself and——No?! What do you mean, *no?*

BILLIE. I don't want to, that's what I mean. *No!* (*Crosses to him.*) In fact, I've never been so *insulted!* (SHE *goes back to desk and resumes collecting.*)

BROCK. (*Softly.*) Well, that's the goddamndest thing I ever heard.

BILLIE. Why?

BROCK. Who the hell are you to say no, if I tell ya?

BILLIE. Don't knock yourself out, you got a lotta surprises coming.

BROCK. Just tell me first.

BILLIE. What?

BROCK. How can *you* not wanna marry *me?*

BILLIE. (*Stopping, looking at him, seriously.*) Well, you're too dumb for one thing. I got a different kinda life in mind, Harry. Entirely. I'm sorry but you just wouldn't fit in.

BROCK. (*Crossing* L. *to sofa.*) Listen, Billie. I don' understand what the hell's happenin'!

BILLIE. (*Resuming at desk.*) *I* do.

BROCK. (*Crossing to* C.) What'd I *do?* What *did* I? All right. I talked rough to you once in a while. Maybe I hit you a couple times. Easy. That a reason to treat me like this? I done good for you, too. Couldn't we straighten it out?

BILLIE. No.

BROCK. Why not?

BILLIE. (*Crossing to him.*) Well, all this stuff I've been reading—and that Paul's been tellin' me—it just mixed me up. But when you hit me before (SHE *points to place in room*) it was like everything *knocked* itself together in my head—and made sense. All of a sudden I realized what it means. How some people are always givin' it and some takin'. And it's not fair. So I'm not gonna let you any more. *Or anybody else!* (*Crosses back to desk, and rummages through it.*)

78

BROCK. (*A new approach.*) Listen, kid. I got an idea. Come on upstairs and I'll calm ya down. (BILLIE *replies by closing a desk drawer with a slam.*) We usta have a pretty good time, remember? (SHE *slams another drawer.*) You wanna come to Florida? (SHE *slams another drawer.*) I think you oughta marry me, don't you? (SHE *slams still another drawer.* HE *is suddenly off the handle.*) Listen, Billie! (BILLIE *crosses below desk to* L. *of sofa.*) I want you to marry me. I don't wanna argue about it. I heard enough. Now you do what I'm tellin' ya or you'll be damn good and sorry.

BILLIE. (*Smiling.*) I'm not scared of you any more, Harry, that's another thing.

BROCK. You're not, huh? (*Moves toward her menacingly.* SHE *is backing away as door buzzer sounds.*)

BILLIE. (*Shouting.*) Come on in! (TWO BELLHOPS *appear,* SHE *points to her room.*) Right up there. (BELLHOPS *start upstairs.*)

BROCK. What the hell's this?

BILLIE. Oh, didn't I tell you? I'm leaving.

BROCK. What?

BILLIE. Yuh, for good.

BROCK. (*To* BELLHOPS.) Wait a second. (THEY *stop.*) Beat it. (BELLHOPS *hesitate.*) Hurry up! (THEY *hurry down.*)

1ST BELLHOP. (*At door.*) Thank you, sir. (BELLHOPS *are gone.*)

BROCK. (*Crossing to* BILLIE.) Let's get *organized* around here. You can't just walk out, cutie. You're in too deep with me. I'm right in the middle of the biggest thing I ever done. Maybe I made a mistake hookin' you in with it—but *you're in!*

BILLIE. Well, I'm not gonna be. I decided.

BROCK. All right, fine. You wanna wash it up?

BILLIE. Yeah.

BROCK. All right, we'll wash it up. I'm too important to monkey around with what *you* think. (HE *shouts upstairs.*) Ed! (*Crossing to desk, looking through papers.*) I'll fix it you can be out of here in no time. You're spoiled. I spoiled you. You're no good to me no more. I was ready to make you a real partner. So you don' want it? So fine. See how you do without me. You don't look like you looked nine years ago. In fact, you look lousy, if you want the truth. I'm glad to get rid of you.

BILLIE. (*Moving toward him.*) And as far as *I'm* concerned —

BROCK. Yeah?

BILLIE. (*Snootily.*) Vice-a!—versa! (DEVERY *comes down.*)

DEVERY. (*To* BILLIE.) You're back. (*To* BROCK.) All set?

79

BROCK. Shut up!

DEVERY. What's the matter?

BROCK. (*Rummaging through desk.*) She's off her nut. We're gonna settle everything up and get 'er the hell outa here.

DEVERY. (*To* BILLIE.) You sure you know what you're doing?

BILLIE. First time in my life I *do* know. (*Sits on sofa, lights cigarette.*)

BROCK. What'd you do with that stuff you wanted 'er to—?

DEVERY. (*Points to coffee table.*) Right there.

BROCK. Where, right there? (DEVERY *looks over at table, then moves to desk.* THEY *search, feverishly.* BILLIE *watches.*)

BILLIE. (*Nonchalantly.*) With blue covers?

DEVERY. (*Opening a drawer.*) Yeah.

BILLIE. Three copies?

BROCK. (*Closing a drawer.*) That's right.

BILLIE. (*Easily.*) I gave 'em to Paul. (BROCK *and* DEVERY *freeze at desk in odd positions, look at each other.*)

BROCK. When?

BILLIE. Just now.

DEVERY. What for?

BILLIE. What d'you think for? To put in the paper, I guess.

BROCK. (*Slams drawer, crosses to her.*) There's some kinda jokes I don't like.

BILLIE. (*Crossing to meet him* C.) It's no joke. Paul says it's the worst swindle since—uh—the *teapot!* (*She shrugs uncertainly.*) Sump'n like that. (*Crosses to front of sofa.* DEVERY *and* BROCK *exchange a horrified look.* BILLIE *turns to them.*) What're you gettin' so white about? You told me yourself it was perfectly all right.

BROCK. (*Furious.*) You double-crossin' little ——

BILLIE. (*Moving to him.*) I don't *see* it like that! If there's a fire and I call the engines—so who am I double-crossing — the *fire?*

DEVERY. (*Going to desk.*) I'd better get Norval.

BROCK. (*Crossing front of desk to up* R.C.) I know who to get. Eddie!!

DEVERY. (*On phone.*) Decatur 9124. (EDDIE *appears.*)

BROCK. (*To* EDDIE.) You know where Verrall's room is?

EDDIE. Sure.

BROCK. Tell 'im to get in here right away.

EDDIE. Right. (*Starts out.* BROCK *follows him.*)

BROCK. Wait a minute. (EDDIE *stops as* BROCK *continues craftily.*)

Tell 'im *Billie* wants 'im. (EDDIE *goes.*)

DEVERY. (*On phone.*) Hello, Norval? Ed. Wake up? . . . Oh, good. I'm over here at Harry's. Can you drop by? Important . . . No, it can't . . . all right. (*Hangs up. Crosses to liquor.*)

BILLIE. (D.L. *at end table.*) Paul's got nothing to do with this. It was my own idea.

BROCK. I'll show you ideas.

BILLIE. (*Crossing to him.*) If you think you can strong-arm him— you're wastin' your time. For a fellow with eye-glasses—he's very —*stubborn!* (SHE *turns and moves away to sofa.* BROCK *crosses to* D.L. *of desk.*)

DEVERY. (*Pouring a drink.*) Oh, dear.

BROCK. If you don't stop bellyachin' get the hell outa here!

DEVERY. We're in trouble, Harry.

BROCK. (*Pointing to* DEVERY'S *drink.*) Is that gonna help?

DEVERY. No. (HE *downs it.*)

BROCK. (*Crossing to* U.R.C.) I'll trim this guy. Watch me.

DEVERY. All right.

BROCK. (*Crossing to* C.) You get in a spot, you fold up. Remind me to give you a heart-to-heart.

DEVERY. (*Crossing to* BROCK.) Be that as it may—if this stuff breaks—nobody'll play with us.

BROCK. So what's to do?

DEVERY. Might be best—under the circumstances—to call off.

BROCK. What?

DEVERY. Let him publish. If nothing happens, he looks silly.

BROCK. What d'you mean nothin' happens? I've spent two months down here and I don' know how much dough. I'm supposed to let all that ride?

DEVERY. If you want to play it safe.

BROCK. (*Crossing* L. *to* R. *of sofa.*) Well, I don't. I want what I'm after.

DEVERY. (*Following him.*) Going to be tough to get.

BROCK. Why? 'Cause some little weasel with eyeglasses gets noisy? I'll cut his tongue out!

DEVERY. (*Face to face.*) Listen, Harry——

BROCK. (*Loud.*) You're chicken!

DEVERY. (*Watching him.*) You think so?

BROCK. I think so!

DEVERY. (*Shouting.*) You're off the handle because it looks like

I've been right and *you've* been wrong.

BROCK. (*Crossing below* DEVERY *to front of desk.*) Talk!

DEVERY. (*Following him.*) I've told you again and again. Get too big you become a target. It's easier to steal diamonds than elephants!

BROCK. (*Turning sharply.*) Shut up! . . . *I'll* handle this.

DEVERY. All right. (*Crosses back to liquor.*)

BROCK. You brought this guy around in the first place. *Remember* that. You're about as much help to me as a boil on the —— (*Stops as* PAUL *comes in, followed by* EDDIE. EDDIE *guards door.* BROCK *moves to* PAUL, *who senses the trap.*) I think you got sump'n by mistake belongs to me.

PAUL. That so?

BROCK. How about it? (PAUL *looks at* BILLIE. BROCK *signals* EDDIE, *who grabs* PAUL'S *arms.* BROCK *frisks him.*)

PAUL. Hey!

BROCK. (*Pointing to sofa.*) Siddown. (PAUL *sits beside* BILLIE.)

PAUL. (*Casually.*) Hello.

BILLIE. (*Politely.*) How've you been?

PAUL. Fine, and you?

BILLIE. Fine.

BROCK. (*To* DEVERY.) Get the stuff outa his room. (DEVERY *starts out.*)

PAUL. Not there, Ed. (DEVERY *stops.*)

BROCK. Where, then? (PAUL *looks at him, smiles, shakes his head.*) All right, if you wanna play it rough, I know how to do that, too. (*Signals* EDDIE, *who locks front door.* BROCK *walks to service wing, bolts door. His determination and purpose strike a kind of terror in every person in the room. Moves back to sofa.*) Now you listen, you two heels. I mean business. I got too much at stake down here. You got sump'n belongs to me. And if you wanna get outa here alive—you're gonna give it back. I'm no blowhard. (*To* BILLIE.) Tell him.

BILLIE. (*To* PAUL, *parrot-like.*) He's no blowhard. (*Then, seriously.*) He's had people killed before. Like once, about six years ago there was a strike at one of his ——

BROCK. Shut up! You ain't gonna be telling *nobody nothin'* pretty soon.

BILLIE. (*Rising to her knees, pointing at* BROCK, *derisively.*) Double negative! (*To* PAUL.) Right?

PAUL. Right! (A pause. EDDIE *is fixing a drink.*)

82

BROCK. You don't seem to be gettin' the idea. You never been in trouble like you're gonna be if you don't do what I'm tellin' ya! (*Starts for* PAUL.)

DEVERY. (*Intercepting him.*) Wait a minute, Harry. There's another way to handle this. (BROCK *turns away, crosses* R. *as* DEVERY *speaks to* PAUL.) I really think you've made a mistake, friend. My advice to you is lay off.

PAUL. And mine to you is stop sticking your noses into my business.

BILLIE. Yeah.

BROCK. Look who's talkin' about stickin' noses. You're the goddamndest butinski I ever run into! (EDDIE *comes down and hands* BROCK *drink.*)

PAUL. . . . told you once before, Harry, that's my job.

BROCK. What? Gettin' in my way? (EDDIE *crosses back to door, leans against it.*)

PAUL. Not exactly.

BROCK. What then? I'd like to know. No kiddin'.

PAUL. To find out what goes on and get it to the people.

BROCK. What people?

PAUL. The people.

BROCK. Never heard of 'em.

BILLIE. You will, Harry, some day. They're gettin' to be more and more well-known all the time.

DEVERY. (*To* PAUL.) What if I told you this whole operation is strictly according to law?

PAUL. Then I'd say the law needs revision.

BROCK. Who're *you?* The *government?*

PAUL. Of course.

BROCK. Since when?

BILLIE. Since—uh—1779! (*To* PAUL.) Right?

PAUL. Right!

BROCK. What? (DEVERY *is back at liquor supply.*)

PAUL. (*Rising, moving to* BROCK.) Of course, I'm the government. What do you think the government is, Harry? A man, a monster, a machine? It's you and me and a few million more. We've got to learn to look after each other.

BROCK. Thanks, I can look after myself.

BILLIE. (*To* PAUL.) He doesn't get it. I think it's because you still talk too fancy. (*To* BROCK.) Look, Harry, the idea is you can only get away with your kind of shenanigans if nobody cares about it.

83

BROCK. I know what I'm doin'. I got my rights same as anybody else.

BILLIE. More! You keep buyin' more and more rights for yourself. (*Buzzer sounds.*)

BROCK. You got nothin' to say to me. (EDDIE *opens door,* HEDGES *comes in,* EDDIE *closes door.* DEVERY *crosses to* L. *of sofa, with drink.*)

HEDGES. Good evening, Eddie! (*Gay, coming into room.*) Well, this is a late little party, isn't it?

BROCK. Shut up!

HEDGES. (C.) What?

BROCK. (*Close to him.*) Don't be so *happy!*

HEDGES. What's the trouble?

DEVERY. Well, our friend Verrall here has—uh—stumbled on a little something. I don't know what he thinks it means.

PAUL. I'll tell you. Just that there may be some connection between Harry's combine and the Senator's amendment.

HEDGES. (*To* PAUL.) Now, just a moment, son. I've got nothing against you young radicals—used to be one myself—but you simply won't be practical. Now, what we're doing is common practice. Done every day. I don't know why you single us out to make a fuss about.

BROCK. Yeah, why?

PAUL. (*To* HEDGES.) Done every day, sir, right. For all I know an undiscovered murder is committed every day. What does *that* prove? All this undercover pressure—bribery—corruption—government between friends. Sure it goes on all the time, and it's tough to crack. Ask me. I've tried for years. You need more than the knowing about it. You've got to have the facts and the figures and most important—the names.

BILLIE. (*Chirping.*) And he's got 'em.

HEDGES. (*Angry.*) You be careful, young man, when you use the word bribery in my presence.

BILLIE. Eighty thousand dollars you got. What word do you want 'im to use? *Tip?* (HEDGES *pales and looks helplessly at* BROCK.)

HEDGES. Harry, I honestly feel —

BROCK. What the hell do I care what you feel? I feel, too.

HEDGES. I can't take any smearing now. It's a bad time.

BROCK. (*Pushing* HEDGES *aside.*) Knock off! (HEDGES *crosses to desk, as* BROCK *moves to* PAUL.) All right, now we all had our little beat around the bush. Let's get down to it. What can we work out?

PAUL. You just heard your lawyer say it was all according to law.

BROCK. Yeah.

PAUL. If that's the case, what's bothering you?

BROCK. I don't like a lotta noise, that's all.

PAUL. I'll be very quiet.

BROCK. What'll you take, Paul?

PAUL. (*Crossing to liquor and pouring drink.*) I'll take a drink, please, if I may.

BROCK. Don't be fancy with me. I never yet met a guy didn't have his price.

PAUL. I have.

BROCK. (*Loud.*) I'm talkin' about big numbers.

BILLIE. (*Louder.*) You and your big numbers! If you don't watch out, you'll be wearin' one across your *chest!* (PAUL *finishes drink.* HEDGES *sits, back of desk, at sea.*)

BROCK. (*To* BILLIE.) I'll get to *you* later. (*To* PAUL.) Make up your mind. There's two ways we can do business. One—you play ball—make it worth your while. Two—you better start watchin' your step. There'll be no place you can walk—no place you can *live*, if you monkey-wrench me! (*A pause.*) What d'you say?

PAUL. I'd like to think it over!

BROCK. All right. You got two minutes! (*Crosses* R. *to front of desk.* PAUL *looks at* BILLIE, *at* BROCK, *then sits quietly. Looks at* BILLIE *again, then at* DEVERY. BILLIE, *too, looks at* DEVERY. BILLIE *looks toward window* L., *seeking an avenue of escape.* PAUL *looks at* EDDIE, *standing near steps of balcony.* EDDIE *and* BROCK *exchange a look.* PAUL *looks at* BROCK, *then at* BILLIE *again.* HE *ponders a moment, looks at his watch.*)

PAUL. Come on, Billie. (PAUL *moves to door.* BILLIE *rises slowly to follow.* BROCK *starts after* PAUL. *Simultaneously,* DEVERY *starts* U.L. *around couch.*)

DEVERY. Wait a minute, Harry! (HE *is crossing to* BROCK.)

HEDGES. (*Rising.*) Now, let's not lose our tempers.

BILLIE. (*Rushing to phone.*) Harry! Harry! (BROCK *reaches* PAUL *and in a sudden inhuman burst, swings him around, grabs him by throat and begins to strangle him.* PAUL *goes to his knees,* BROCK *hangs on.*)

DEVERY. (*In a panic.*) Cut it out! Harry!

HEDGES. Oh, my God!

BILLIE. (*Picks up phone and screams.*) Operator! Operator! (ED-

DIE *gets to her.* THEY *struggle for phone noisily.* DEVERY *and* HEDGES *are desperately attempting to prevent murder. Finally, they tear* BROCK *loose.* BILLIE *rushes to* PAUL *to help him. His glasses have been knocked off and his clothes are torn. He is groggy.* DEVERY *throws* BROCK *onto sofa, where he sits, spent and subdued.*)

DEVERY. (*To* BROCK.) You goddamn fool! Where the hell do you think you are? Can't you see all this muscle stuff is a thing of the past? You cut it out, or you'll be a thing of the past, too. (*Crosses to liquor.*)

BROCK. I got mad!

PAUL. (*Coming down to him.*) Who are *you* to get mad, you big baboon? You ought to be grateful you're allowed to walk around free.

BROCK. (*Warning.*) You don't know me good enough for that kinda talk.

PAUL. (*Losing his temper.*) I know you. I've seen your kind down here for years. What the hell do you guys want, anyway? You've *got* all the oil and all the lumber and steel and coal—what do you want now—all the people? All the laws?

BROCK. (*Rising.*) Don't blow your top! (*Crosses to* PAUL.) I'm still ready to do business. How's a hundred grand?

PAUL. (*Turning away, crossing to* L. *of desk.*) A hundred grand is beautiful—but I can't do it.

BROCK. Why not? (*A pause.*)

PAUL. (*Turning to him.*) My wife wouldn't like it. (*Another pause.*)

BILLIE. (*Softly.*) She certainly wouldn't!

BROCK. (*To* PAUL.) All right, then, what's *your* idea?

PAUL. Nothing—no idea—I'm just trying to show you that—look, there's a difference between junk and—legislation's not *meant* for buying and selling.

BILLIE. "This country with its institutions belongs to the people who *inhibit* it!"

PAUL. (*Correcting her.*) "—inhabit!"

BILLIE. "—inhabit it!"

BROCK. What the hell you two battin' about? I don' see what I'm doin' so wrong. This is America, ain't it? Where's all this free enterprise they're always talkin' about?

DEVERY. (*Toasting.*) To free enterprise! (*Drinks.*)

BROCK. (*To* PAUL.) You're just sore because I made good and you

86

ain't. Everybody had the same chance as me—all them kids I usta know—so where are they now?

BILLIE. (*Coming to him.*) No place. Because you beat 'em out, like you said. You always wanna hold everybody down so you can get it all for yourself. That's why there's like my father—and like me. I wanted—and he couldn't give me—so I wind up with an empty head and with you.

BROCK. I always did what I want and I'm always gonna.

BILLIE. Try it! (*Moves to* PAUL, *stands beside him.*)

BROCK. Who's gonna stop me?

BILLIE. (*With a gesture.*) Us two.

BROCK. (*Contemptuously.*) Youse two? Don't make me split a gut. Be some fine day where a hundred-and-a-quarter-a-week hick and a broad ain't been off her end in ten years can stop *me*. (HE *turns and sees* DEVERY.) What the hell *you* standin' around like a deef and dumby? What do I pay you for? Say something!

DEVERY. All right. I'll say something.

BROCK. Well?

DEVERY. They're right. (EDDIE *is getting* BROCK *another drink.*)

BROCK. Who the hell's side you *on*?

EDDIE. (*Handing* BROCK *drink.*) Rye ginger ale.

BROCK. Who asked you? Butt out! (*Hands glass back to* EDDIE, *who retreats.*)

PAUL. (*Crossing to* BROCK.) Maybe another time, Harry, not now. And if you're going to try again—do it fast. It gets harder all the time—people get wiser—they hear more—they read more—they talk more. When enough of them know enough—that'll be the end of you.

BROCK. Don't worry about *me*.

PAUL. I do, though. I worry like hell. I stay up nights. When you live in Washington, it's enough to break your heart. You see a perfect piece of machinery—the democratic structure—and somebody's always tampering with it and trying to make it hit the jackpot.

DEVERY. (*Toasting.*) To the jackpot. (*Drinks.*)

BROCK. I'm no gambler. I'm a business man.

PAUL. You certainly are, but you tried the wrong business.

BILLIE. (*To* BROCK, *from behind* PAUL.) When you steal from the government, you're stealin' from yourself, you dumb ox! (SHE *flinches from the expected reaction, which fails to materialize.*)

BROCK. (*To them both.*) Do what you want! I'm goin' right ahead.

87

(*Moves away from them to front of desk.*)

BILLIE. Wait a minute! I'll tell you where you're goin'.

BROCK. (*Turning.*) You?!

BILLIE. (*Crossing to him.*) Sure. In this whole thing—I guess you forgot about me—about how I'm a partner? Ed once told me—a hundred and twenty-six different yards I own.

DEVERY. Control.

BILLIE. (*Closer to* BROCK.) Same thing. So here's how it's gonna be. I don't want 'em, I don't want anything of yours—or to *do* with you. So I'm gonna sign 'em all back —

BROCK. All right.

BILLIE. Only not all at once—just one at a time—*one a year!* (BROCK *is stunned.* BILLIE *crosses to* PAUL, *then turns back to* BROCK.) But you better behave yourself—because if you don't I'm gonna let go on everything. For what you've done even since I've known you only, I'll bet you could be put in jail for about nine hundred years. You'd be a pretty old man when you got out. (*Crosses to chair* R. *of door, picks up hat and bag.*)

BROCK. (*Dazed.*) What's goin' on around here?

DEVERY. A revolution?

BILLIE. (*To* PAUL.) Come on, Paul. (*To* BROCK.) I'll send for my things. (PAUL *and* BILLIE *start for door.*)

BROCK. (*Moving to* BILLIE.) You little crumb—you'll be sorry for this day—wait and see. Go on—go with him—you ain't got a chance. If I ever seen somebody outsmart themself, it's *you.*

BILLIE. (*To the room.*) Goodbye, all. (SHE *moves,* PAUL *follows.*)

BROCK. (*To* PAUL.) And you!

PAUL. Me?

BROCK. Yeah—you're fired!

PAUL. I'm sorry, Harry. I enjoyed working for you. (*Turns and stands behind* BILLIE, *who is at door, still guarded by* EDDIE.)

BILLIE. (*Quietly to* EDDIE.) Open up!

EDDIE. (*To* BROCK.) All right, Harry?

BILLIE. (*Yelling in imitation of* BROCK.) *Do what I'm tellin' ya!* (EDDIE *jumps, opens door quickly.* BILLIE *turns, smiles sweetly at* BROCK *and goes, followed by* PAUL. EDDIE *closes door.* DEVERY *pours himself a drink.* BROCK *is incredulous.*)

BROCK. (*Trying to laugh it off.*) How d'you like that? *He* coulda had a hundred grand—and *she* coulda had *me!* So they both wind up with *nothin'!* (*A hollow laugh.* HE *looks at door.*) Dumb chump.

HEDGES. Yes.

BROCK. (*Starting up stairs.*) Crazy broad.

HEDGES. Quite right.

DEVERY. (*Toasting, glass held high.*) To all the dumb chumps and all the crazy broads,—(BROCK *stops midway up stairs and turns back to listen*) past, present and future—who thirst for knowledge—-and search for truth—who fight for justice—and civilize each other—and make it so tough for sons-of-bitches (*To.* HEDGES.) like you—(*To* BROCK.) and you—and me.(*Drinks.*)

CURTAIN

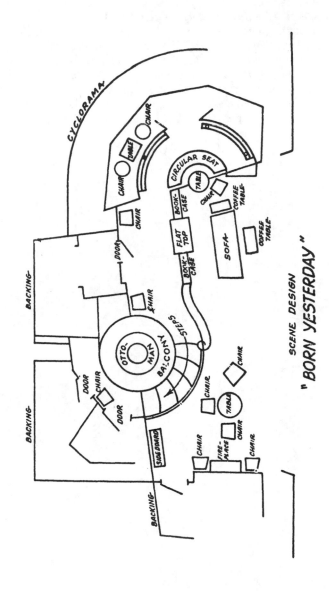

SCENE DESIGN
"BORN YESTERDAY"

PROPERTY LIST

The property list used for the Broadway production is long and elaborate; the list that appears below is considerably simplified. Since each group will, of course, use its judgment as to how elaborate the entire set is to be, it is not advisable to compile a *complete* property list. Many decorations and properties used in the original production are elaborate and while a good many are fundamentally necessary, others were introduced chiefly for purposes of atmosphere and mood. It is believed that the following list will suffice:

Several highball and shot glasses

Several bottles of whiskey and a few of soda and ginger ale

Several cigarette boxes with cigarettes and matches

Many ash trays

(For maid's cleaning outfit) Linen bag, broom, dusters, pillow cases, sheets, towels

(For barber's kit) Hair brush, razor, towels, brushless shaving cream, barber's bib

(For manicurist basket) Towel, nail nippers, scissors, emery boards, etc.

(For bootblack kit) Cloths, brush, shoe polish

Bellhop's key ring around his neck, extra key on chain

Few sheets of yellow paper and pencil

One copy "New Republic"

Several books (a few for tearing up)

A large number of magazines and newspapers

One newspaper with red crayon markings

Red grease pencil

Traffic ticket

Attaché case with blotter & legal papers

Manila envelope with legal papers

Fountain pen (Devery)

6 to 10 suitcases & travelling bags

Large candy box with silk ribbon

Long-handle hair brush (Billie)

Small card in envelope (in bunch of flowers)

Ice bucket with ice and tongs

Cigar humidor

Two packs playing cards with score pad and pencil

Key

Money—bills and change

2 pairs eyeglasses

4 or 5 album records

Large paper map

6 Airmail envelopes, stamped & cancelled

1 large brown envelope, stamped & cancelled, holding 4 legal documents

1 small glass pitcher with water

1 large and 1 small dictionary

Several sharpened pencils

Tea Service with cups, saucers, spoons, bowl, pitcher

Letter in envelope, addressed.

Small black note-book with pencil in it

Several newspaper clippings

Blotter, memo pad, letter opener, desk pen and stand, all on desk

3 large check books

Bundle of letters with rubber band around it

4 crumpled sheets from yellow paper pad

NEW PLAYS

★ **MOTHERHOOD OUT LOUD by Leslie Ayvazian, Brooke Berman, David Cale, Jessica Goldberg, Beth Henley, Lameece Issaq, Claire LaZebnik, Lisa Loomer, Michele Lowe, Marco Pennette, Theresa Rebeck, Luanne Rice, Annie Weisman and Cheryl L. West, conceived by Susan R. Rose and Joan Stein.** When entrusting the subject of motherhood to such a dazzling collection of celebrated American writers, what results is a joyous, moving, hilarious, and altogether thrilling theatrical event. "Never fails to strike both the funny bone and the heart." *—BackStage.* "Packed with wisdom, laughter, and plenty of wry surprises." *—TheaterMania.* [1M, 3W] ISBN: 978-0-8222-2589-8

★ **COCK by Mike Bartlett.** When John takes a break from his boyfriend, he accidentally meets the girl of his dreams. Filled with guilt and indecision, he decides there is only one way to straighten this out. "[A] brilliant and blackly hilarious feat of provocation." *—Independent.* "A smart, prickly and rewarding view of sexual and emotional confusion." *—Evening Standard.* [3M, 1W] ISBN: 978-0-8222-2766-3

★ **F. Scott Fitzgerald's THE GREAT GATSBY adapted for the stage by Simon Levy.** Jay Gatsby, a self-made millionaire, passionately pursues the elusive Daisy Buchanan. Nick Carraway, a young newcomer to Long Island, is drawn into their world of obsession, greed and danger. "Levy's combination of narration, dialogue and action delivers most of what is best in the novel." *—Seattle Post-Intelligencer.* "A beautifully crafted interpretation of the 1925 novel which defined the Jazz Age." *—London Free Press.* [5M, 4W] ISBN: 978-0-8222-2727-4

★ **LONELY, I'M NOT by Paul Weitz.** At an age when most people are discovering what they want to do with their lives, Porter has been married and divorced, earned seven figures as a corporate "ninja," and had a nervous breakdown. It's been four years since he's had a job or a date, and he's decided to give life another shot. "Critic's pick!" *—NY Times.* "An enjoyable ride." *—NY Daily News.* [3M, 3W] ISBN: 978-0-8222-2734-2

★ **ASUNCION by Jesse Eisenberg.** Edgar and Vinny are not racist. In fact, Edgar maintains a blog condemning American imperialism, and Vinny is three-quarters into a Ph.D. in Black Studies. When Asuncion becomes their new roommate, the boys have a perfect opportunity to demonstrate how open-minded they truly are. "Mr. Eisenberg writes lively dialogue that strikes plenty of comic sparks." *—NY Times.* "An almost ridiculously enjoyable portrait of slacker trauma among would-be intellectuals." *—Newsday.* [2M, 2W] ISBN: 978-0-8222-2630-7

DRAMATISTS PLAY SERVICE, INC.
440 Park Avenue South, New York, NY 10016 212-683-8960 Fax 212-213-1539
postmaster@dramatists.com   www.dramatists.com

NEW PLAYS

★ **THE PICTURE OF DORIAN GRAY by Roberto Aguirre-Sacasa, based on the novel by Oscar Wilde.** Preternaturally handsome Dorian Gray has his portrait painted by his college classmate Basil Hallwood. When their mutual friend Henry Wotton offers to include it in a show, Dorian makes a fateful wish—that his portrait should grow old instead of him—and strikes an unspeakable bargain with the devil. [5M, 2W] ISBN: 978-0-8222-2590-4

★ **THE LYONS by Nicky Silver.** As Ben Lyons lies dying, it becomes clear that he and his wife have been at war for many years, and his impending demise has brought no relief. When they're joined by their children all efforts at a sentimental goodbye to the dying patriarch are soon abandoned. "Hilariously frank, clear-sighted, compassionate and forgiving." –*NY Times.* "Mordant, dark and rich." –*Associated Press.* [3M, 3W] ISBN: 978-0-8222-2659-8

★ **STANDING ON CEREMONY by Mo Gaffney, Jordan Harrison, Moisés Kaufman, Neil LaBute, Wendy MacLeod, José Rivera, Paul Rudnick, and Doug Wright, conceived by Brian Shnipper.** Witty, warm and occasionally wacky, these plays are vows to the blessings of equality, the universal challenges of relationships and the often hilarious power of love. "CEREMONY puts a human face on a hot-button issue and delivers laughter and tears rather than propaganda." –*BackStage.* [3M, 3W] ISBN: 978-0-8222-2654-3

★ **ONE ARM by Moisés Kaufman, based on the short story and screenplay by Tennessee Williams.** Ollie joins the Navy and becomes the lightweight boxing champion of the Pacific Fleet. Soon after, he loses his arm in a car accident, and he turns to hustling to survive. "[A] fast, fierce, brutally beautiful stage adaptation." –*NY Magazine.* "A fascinatingly lurid, provocative and fatalistic piece of theater." –*Variety.* [7M, 1W] ISBN: 978-0-8222-2564-5

★ **AN ILIAD by Lisa Peterson and Denis O'Hare.** A modern-day retelling of Homer's classic. Poetry and humor, the ancient tale of the Trojan War and the modern world collide in this captivating theatrical experience. "Shocking, glorious, primal and deeply satisfying." –*Time Out NY.* "Explosive, altogether breathtaking." –*Chicago Sun-Times.* [1M] ISBN: 978-0-8222-2687-1

★ **THE COLUMNIST by David Auburn.** At the height of the Cold War, Joe Alsop is the nation's most influential journalist, beloved, feared and courted by the Washington world. But as the '60s dawn and America undergoes dizzying change, the intense political dramas Joe is embroiled in become deeply personal as well. "Intensely satisfying." –*Bloomberg News.* [5M, 2W] ISBN: 978-0-8222-2699-4

DRAMATISTS PLAY SERVICE, INC.
440 Park Avenue South, New York, NY 10016   212-683-8960   Fax 212-213-1539
postmaster@dramatists.com   www.dramatists.com

NEW PLAYS

★ **BENGAL TIGER AT THE BAGHDAD ZOO by Rajiv Joseph.** The lives of two American Marines and an Iraqi translator are forever changed by an encounter with a quick-witted tiger who haunts the streets of war-torn Baghdad. "[A] boldly imagined, harrowing and surprisingly funny drama." –*NY Times*. "Tragic yet darkly comic and highly imaginative." –*CurtainUp*. [5M, 2W] ISBN: 978-0-8222-2565-2

★ **THE PITMEN PAINTERS by Lee Hall, inspired by a book by William Feaver.** Based on the triumphant true story, a group of British miners discover a new way to express themselves and unexpectedly become art-world sensations. "Excitingly ambiguous, in-the-moment theater." –*NY Times*. "Heartfelt, moving and deeply politicized." –*Chicago Tribune*. [5M, 2W] ISBN: 978-0-8222-2507-2

★ **RELATIVELY SPEAKING by Ethan Coen, Elaine May and Woody Allen.** In TALKING CURE, Ethan Coen uncovers the sort of insanity that can only come from family. Elaine May explores the hilarity of passing in GEORGE IS DEAD. In HONEYMOON MOTEL, Woody Allen invites you to the sort of wedding day you won't forget. "Firecracker funny." –*NY Times*. "A rollicking good time." –*New Yorker*. [8M, 7W] ISBN: 978-0-8222-2394-8

★ **SONS OF THE PROPHET by Stephen Karam.** If to live is to suffer, then Joseph Douaihy is more alive than most. With unexplained chronic pain and the fate of his reeling family on his shoulders, Joseph's health, sanity, and insurance premium are on the line. "Explosively funny." –*NY Times*. "At once deep, deft and beautifully made." –*New Yorker*. [5M, 3W] ISBN: 978-0-8222-2597-3

★ **THE MOUNTAINTOP by Katori Hall.** A gripping reimagination of events the night before the assassination of the civil rights leader Dr. Martin Luther King, Jr. "An ominous electricity crackles through the opening moments." –*NY Times*. "[A] thrilling, wild, provocative flight of magical realism." –*Associated Press*. "Crackles with theatricality and a humanity more moving than sainthood." –*NY Newsday*. [1M, 1W] ISBN: 978-0-8222-2603-1

★ **ALL NEW PEOPLE by Zach Braff.** Charlie is 35, heartbroken, and just wants some time away from the rest of the world. Long Beach Island seems to be the perfect escape until his solitude is interrupted by a motley parade of misfits who show up and change his plans. "Consistently and sometimes sensationally funny." –*NY Times*. "A morbidly funny play about the trendy new existential condition of being young, adorable, and miserable." –*Variety*. [2M, 2W] ISBN: 978-0-8222-2562-1

DRAMATISTS PLAY SERVICE, INC.
440 Park Avenue South, New York, NY 10016 212-683-8960 Fax 212-213-1539
postmaster@dramatists.com www.dramatists.com

NEW PLAYS

★ **CLYBOURNE PARK by Bruce Norris.** WINNER OF THE 2011 PULITZER PRIZE AND 2012 TONY AWARD. Act One takes place in 1959 as community leaders try to stop the sale of a home to a black family. Act Two is set in the same house in the present day as the now predominantly African-American neighborhood battles to hold its ground. "Vital, sharp-witted and ferociously smart." –*NY Times.* "A theatrical treasure…Indisputably, uproariously funny." –*Entertainment Weekly.* [4M, 3W] ISBN: 978-0-8222-2697-0

★ **WATER BY THE SPOONFUL by Quiara Alegría Hudes.** WINNER OF THE 2012 PULITZER PRIZE. A Puerto Rican veteran is surrounded by the North Philadelphia demons he tried to escape in the service. "This is a very funny, warm, and yes uplifting play." –*Hartford Courant.* "The play is a combination poem, prayer and app on how to cope in an age of uncertainty, speed and chaos." –*Variety.* [4M, 3W] ISBN: 978-0-8222-2716-8

★ **RED by John Logan.** WINNER OF THE 2010 TONY AWARD. Mark Rothko has just landed the biggest commission in the history of modern art. But when his young assistant, Ken, gains the confidence to challenge him, Rothko faces the agonizing possibility that his crowning achievement could also become his undoing. "Intense and exciting." –*NY Times.* "Smart, eloquent entertainment." –*New Yorker.* [2M] ISBN: 978-0-8222-2483-9

★ **VENUS IN FUR by David Ives.** Thomas, a beleaguered playwright/director, is desperate to find an actress to play Vanda, the female lead in his adaptation of the classic sadomasochistic tale *Venus in Fur.* "Ninety minutes of good, kinky fun." –*NY Times.* "A fast-paced journey into one man's entrapment by a clever, vengeful female." –*Associated Press.* [1M, 1W] ISBN: 978-0-8222-2603-1

★ **OTHER DESERT CITIES by Jon Robin Baitz.** Brooke returns home to Palm Springs after a six-year absence and announces that she is about to publish a memoir dredging up a pivotal and tragic event in the family's history—a wound they don't want reopened. "Leaves you feeling both moved and gratifyingly sated." –*NY Times.* "A genuine pleasure." –*NY Post.* [2M, 3W] ISBN: 978-0-8222-2605-5

★ **TRIBES by Nina Raine.** Billy was born deaf into a hearing family and adapts brilliantly to his family's unconventional ways, but it's not until he meets Sylvia, a young woman on the brink of deafness, that he finally understands what it means to be understood. "A smart, lively play." –*NY Times.* "[A] bright and boldly provocative drama." –*Associated Press.* [3M, 2W] ISBN: 978-0-8222-2751-9

DRAMATISTS PLAY SERVICE, INC.
440 Park Avenue South, New York, NY 10016 212-683-8960 Fax 212-213-1539
postmaster@dramatists.com   www.dramatists.com